Contents

Living Prayer

Mother M. Angelica

SERVANT BOOKS
Ann Arbor, Michigan

Published by Servant Books
Box 8617
Ann Arbor, Michigan 48107

Cover photo: Ed Cooper
Book design by John B. Leidy

Excerpts from *The Jerusalem Bible*, copyright © 1966
by Darton, Longman & Todd, Ltd. and Doubleday &
Company, Inc.
Reprinted by permission of the publisher.

Printed in the United States of America
ISBN 0-89283-280-0

85 86 87 88 89 10 9 8 7 6 5 4 3 2

ONE

The First Christians

THROUGHOUT ALL THE EPISTLES and Acts, one gets the impression that the first Christians ate, drank, slept, talked, and argued about nothing else but their beliefs and their Jesus. When they became engrossed in the affairs of the world and returned to their old ways, the sacred writers reproved them severely.

These first Christians used every moment of their lives to change themselves into images of Jesus. When they were not talking to Jesus in prayer, their lives manifested the virtues of Jesus.

They did not permit themselves the self-indulgence of living in the past or future. They never knew when their newfound faith would demand the sacrifice of home, land, and life. They were determined to live every moment of their lives for and with Jesus.

They failed, as we all do, but when they did, they rose up from those failures with courage and love. This is not to say that they were perfect and that modern-day Christians are not; it is only to show how they lived in their present moment amid great trials and difficulties, in the hope that we may regain what we have lost and begin anew to live a life of fervor as they did.

Perhaps by looking at them we may observe how they prayed without ceasing in their hearts, minds, and souls.

The presence of Jesus in their souls was a glorious experience to the first Christians. It was not always a "feeling" experience, but it was a constant, continuous faith experience—an awareness of God dwelling in their souls and in their neighbor. The painful circumstances of life were merely opportunities for them to find their Lord, and to rejoice that they were counted worthy to suffer for his name's sake (Acts 5:41).

Throughout the epistles and Acts, we find these first Christians imbued with a spirit of awareness and mission—awareness of God's presence within them and a realization that they were to manifest that presence to their neighbor.

To do this, they had to pray, to commune with the Master constantly. Their whole being was to change into something wonderful, into a son of God. Every day was a challenge, an opportunity to grow into the image they loved so much.

The question in the minds of Christians today is: "How did they do it?" It is obvious, from the heroic deeds they accomplished, the pain they suffered, and the martyrdom they endured, that they had something we lack.

They had the Spirit—but so do we.

They had the Eucharist—but so do we.

They had men who taught them the Word of God—but so do we.

They had communal worship—but so do we.

They prayed without ceasing—but we do not.

They possessed a faith vision—but we do not.

They began in their prayer life where most of us end. They had no degrees of prayer to attain, no definitions to guide them, no steps to follow. They never knew the difference between vocal prayer and the prayer of union. They seemed to have little knowledge of ways and means but they had a great experience with God as Father.

They had a simple humility that acknowledged their sins, and reached out to Jesus as Lord and Savior. They buried themselves, their personalities, their possessions, goals, and desires—buried them in Jesus. Looking at themselves with honesty, they cried out to God, "Abba, Father."

It would be centuries before men could define what these first Christians possessed. It would take centuries more to explain the intricacies of a life of prayer and union with God. But to these first fruits of redemption, life was a challenge and a continuous prayer—a goal that love would attain and perseverance acquire.

They had only one desire: to be like Jesus in their everyday life. They arrived at this goal through the power and grace of the Holy Spirit and persevering effort in attaining the prayer of imitation.

This was the good news to be proclaimed to the world. They were called to be like Jesus and thereby prove that Jesus was Lord.

We will look at the way they kept Jesus in their hearts and minds and grew in grace moment to moment.

The Imitation of Jesus

The words of Jesus were not merely the foundation of their faith but also the maxims by which they lived. They were to be imitators of their divine model and count it a blessing to suffer for his name. His words found a home in their hearts. That home was a place in which their spirits grew into the likeness of Jesus.

They were careful that the house was swept clean of the dirt of sin and the dust of selfishness. It was not filled with the cluttering superfluities that make it impossible to move about with ease.

They began their imitation of Jesus by emptying themselves of all the excess baggage that burdened them.

Their material possessions did not weigh them down, because they shared everything they had with one another. In sharing, they were not deprived, and even when some of the widows of the Hellenists were overlooked, their complaint led to a fairer distribution (Acts 4:34, 6:1-6).

These first Christians realized that inner burdens and attachments were the real possessions that must be relinquished for the good of the kingdom and their own holiness. Their new lives were centered upon the goal of emptying themselves and being filled with God.

"Free your minds, then, of encumbrances," St. Peter told them, "control them and put your trust in nothing but the grace that will be given you. . . . You must be scrupulously careful as long as you are living away from your home" (1 Pt 1:13, 17).

Their real home was heaven, so this world and everything in it took on the appearance of a temporary residence—a place away from home—an inn on a journey. With this concept in mind and the divine promises in their hearts, they became pilgrims and travelers who were on a journey. Like all journeys, it took on the aspect of a challenge and an adventure. They vied with one another, not in worldly pursuits, but in the imitation of Jesus.

"I urge you, my dear people," St. Peter exhorted them, "while you are visitors and pilgrims, to keep yourselves free from selfish passions that attack the soul" (1 Pt 2:11). Life began to have meaning as they listened to Paul say that the prophets of old "were only strangers and nomads on earth . . . in search of their real homeland. . . . they were longing for a better homeland, their heavenly homeland" (Heb 11:13-15).

The realization that this world was not "home" gave the Christians a whole new kind of life and way of living. They not only realized this truth but were told where "home" was and how to prepare for it. They did not have the struggle for detachment that we have because in the realization that earth was not home, everything they clung to suddenly seemed unimportant.

This detachment did not make them indifferent. No, they worked, and worked hard, were concerned about others and shared what they possessed with them. They were called to work for a living and to be hospitable (Rom 12:13). They lived a full life but were never constrained or tied down by what they accomplished or the demands of life made on them.

They were free and that freedom was paid for by the precious blood of Jesus (1 Pt 1:18). Jesus told them, "If you make my word your home you will indeed be my disciples, you will learn the truth and the truth will make you free" (Jn 8:32).

The truth that God lived in these souls through the power of his Spirit and that heaven was their true home made these people new men and women. Their minds thought in a new way; their actions were Christlike; their motives were pure; their souls were clothed in a faith that moved the mountains of evil around them.

Their whole lives suddenly had a purpose and a mission. They saw God everywhere and in everything that happened to them. Most of all they now had someone to follow—a perfect model by whom to measure themselves.

Though the gospels had not been written, each Christian would write down those words of Jesus that appealed to him, memorize them, and then live by them. Peter and Paul began to write letters that explained the faith; these letters were copied and passed around as precious treasures.

Jesus had told them that they should dance for joy when they were persecuted because their reward was great in heaven (Lk 21:12). That one statement gave meaning to their lives. For centuries the world experienced pain and suffering without meaning or purpose. Human life was expendable and compassion was considered a weakness. Sickness and injustice were everywhere and the law of the land was to survive no matter what the cost.

The Source of Strength

They needed a constant source of strength and they found that source in prayer. Prayer to the first Christians was like breathing; it was part of their moment to moment existence. It was not a tedious obligation but an outpouring of the heart to someone very close—someone living in their very souls.

Their prayer was a desire to be like Jesus; they did not separate their lives from prayer. Prayer became such a part of life that it was woven throughout it like golden threads in a tapestry.

To think of Jesus was to pray. To love Jesus was to pray. To talk of Jesus was to pray. And to be like Jesus was to glorify the Father.

Jesus told them, "It is to the glory of my Father that you should bear fruit, and then you will be my disciples" (Jn 15:8). To give glory to the Father was the highest form of prayer. To be a disciple was the best way to show their gratitude for redemption.

These Christians studied the life of Jesus and saw what he did and how he acted under every circumstance. They realized that "because he has himself been through temptation he is able to help others who are tempted" (Heb 2:18).

"That is why," St. Paul told them, "all you who are holy brothers and have had the same heavenly call should turn your minds to Jesus" (Heb 3:1). This was the secret of their ability to pray without ceasing. In everything they did, they turned their minds to Jesus.

They were to "keep their minds constantly occupied in doing good works" because they were now sons of God and brothers of Jesus (Ti 3:8).

"You see," St. Paul reminded them, "God's grace has been revealed . . . and taught us that what we have to do is to give up everything that does not lead us to God, and all our worldly ambitions; we must be self-restrained and live good and religious lives in this present world" (Ti 2:12, 13).

They had to give up their old ways and adopt new ones. The realization of heaven as homeland detached them from their possessions, and the realization that the Father sent his Son to redeem them detached them from themselves. They thought of nothing but the new life and put off the old like a torn garment.

The words of Paul ran through their minds over and over, "For anyone who is in Christ, there is a new creation; the old creation has gone, and now the new one is here" (2 Cor 5:17). "We groan as we wait with longing to put on our heavenly home" (2 Cor 5:2).

These two thoughts gave them wings to fly into the arms of God. No longer fearful of the future, no longer burdened with their past, they lived the present moment like Jesus, their model and Lord.

They were "ambassadors of Christ," his "letter to the world," sons of the Father, and witnesses that Jesus was Lord. They belonged to God and proved they were sons "by great fortitude in times of suffering . . . hardship, and distress . . . by our purity, knowledge, patience and kindness; by a spirit of holiness, by a love free of affectation . . . by being prepared for honor or disgrace, blame or praise" (2 Cor 5:4-8).

They combined all these goals into one goal—to be like Jesus. All the power of their wills was geared in one direction—to be like Jesus. They had only one desire and only one ambition—to be like Jesus.

To Be Like Jesus

They would be humble, because he told them to learn from him, for he was meek and humble of heart. They would not worry, because he told them to trust the Father who cared for them. They would leave their burdens to God, because he told them not to judge. They would look for the invisible reality behind life's sufferings, because he gave them beatitudes to insure their joy. They would never feel lonely, because he told them the Spirit would live in them and bring to their minds his words. They would share with one another and make hospitality their special boast because he told them to love one another as he loved them. They knew in the depths of their souls that God loved them with a tremendous love, and they had to return that love in the best way possible.

"You were darkness once," Paul told them, "but now you are light in the Lord; be like children of light, for the effects of the light are seen in complete goodness and right living and truth" (Eph 5:8-9).

The power of his death and resurrection made children of darkness into beacons of light. The power of his Spirit changed their lives and made them radiate goodness. Their mission was to expose darkness "by contrast" (Eph 5:12).

They did not need to preach Jesus—they were Jesus. They took upon themselves his beautiful qualities, enhanced their own personalities by modeling them on his, and then led others to the Father by their joy and love.

They were told to "imitate God . . . and follow Christ by loving as he loved" (Eph 5:1), and that imitation constituted a prayer style that was before unknown. Their prayer life before was one of fearsome homage. The words they spoke were measured and reverent, mixed with a feeling of inferiority and inadequacy. Now they knew Jesus, God's own Son. They possessed his very Spirit; they were heirs with him of an eternal life, and this realization made their whole lives a prayer of imitation.

In everything they said or did, the words of Paul renewed their determination to be like Jesus. "Do not model yourselves on the behavior of the world around you," he said, "but let your behavior change, modeled by your new mind" (Rom 12:2). "In your minds you must be the same as Christ Jesus" (Phil 2:5).

Their lives were made new by thinking like Jesus and this "spiritual revolution" changed their actions, their attitudes, their goals, and their desires. Their lives became a prayer, for every moment was colored by the longing to be like their God.

Jesus said that with him in them they would bear much fruit, but without him they could do nothing. They must have found that statement difficult to understand; every human being desires to be himself and wants his personality to be completely his own. It must have taken them a little time to realize what it all meant. When they compared themselves to Jesus, they became more and more aware of the vast difference between themselves and Jesus.

They observed his actions in every situation, heard or read his words of comfort and encouragement, and saw him triumph over his enemies. They realized that imitating Jesus was not a matter of being molded into one communal pattern. It was not a matter of giving up one's personality or will; it was a matter of using one's free will, of choosing to be humble enough to know that he had something better to give, and of loving him enough to want to be like him.

It was a choice one made to drink at the fountain of living water, to be filled with the grace that comes from God alone, and to develop one's natural good qualities into Godlike actions. It was not slavery, it was freedom. To imitate Jesus meant replacing a mere vacuum with an emptiness that was constantly being filled, a narrowness that was continually being expanded.

Their lives were so changed that everyone recognized them as Christians. Their desires, attitudes, speech, actions, and opinions were all changed in a way that attracted pagans from every nation.

Yes, their lives were one beautiful prayer, always changing in its expression, always harmonizing with life situations, always in tune with the melody they heard from the heart of God.

TWO

Total Prayer

THE FIRST CHRISTIANS soon learned that there were many ways of expressing themselves to God. There were times they spoke to God about his beauty, or about their needs; that was conversational prayer. They spoke to him silently in their thoughts, and as they spoke to him, they realized he answered them. He answered in the same way they spoke—by thought.

Many times they were afraid as they were hunted like animals, and that very fear reached up to God for help. At times like these they felt a surge of courage revive their spirits, and the words of Jesus ran through their minds. Then they wondered why they had been so afraid. God had spoken to them, and his word was proved by power.

At other times they had to fight the enemy within. They realized they needed mental discipline to control the spiritual faculties that caused such havoc in their souls. They would quiet their minds by using their memories to recall some incident in the life of Jesus. This effort calmed any resentment that might be deposited in that faculty. To ensure that their thought of Jesus would take hold, they would use their imaginations to picture the scene and suddenly it was as if they were really there. They would feel the sentiments of his heart in that situation and begin to apply them to themselves.

To the first Christians this kind of prayer was a "Jesus experience," but to us it is a "meditation." To them it was a heart experience; to us it is a mind experience. To them it was a faith vision resulting in a change of life; to us it is an intellectual exercise resulting in speculations and theological arguments. They prayed and changed themselves; we pray and change things.

Some worldly Christians do not live and breathe Jesus. Their prayer life is limited to conversational prayer when in need, formal prayer when they cannot think of what to say to God, and sometimes mental prayer when their souls are at peace.

All these forms of prayer are limited to a time and a place. They are part of our prayer life, but only a part. If that life is fed only by these forms of prayer, Jesus will come and go in our lives according to our needs, spare time, and abilities. He will not be our constant companion and intimate friend. We shall never pray without ceasing.

Prayer of the Heart

The first Christians soon realized that if they were to persevere in the new life they were chosen to live, they had to love intensely. Love made Christianity so different from any other religion.

Man is a being of emotion; to live only in faith and hope would be to live in a desert with light and air but no warmth. Man needs incentive and drive to propel him out of darkness into light, or better still, to radiate light in the midst of darkness.

Life was difficult at best. Though Christianity gave them peace within, it created havoc around them. It made some men examine their consciences and showed them up for what they really were—false and tyrannical. It takes a great man to see himself and change, but the world was sometimes ruled by small men—men who rebelled at the sight of themselves. They struck out at these Christians with a fury that only hatred could produce.

These Christians had to keep themselves above every situation that tended to drag their souls down and make them want to retaliate at anger and hatred. They had to nourish and maintain within themselves a never-ending source of love. They had to feed their souls with life-giving water.

Faith and Love

Jesus had sent the Advocate to dwell in their souls and they were determined that nothing would interfere with that union. Every moment of their lives had to be used to grow in the image of Jesus.

Faith gave them a belief and hope a goal, but to keep both alive and active they needed to love.

Faith settled the doubts in their intellects and hope calmed their emotions, but they needed love to give them the endurance to persevere.

Faith told them what they believed and hope told them why, but it was love that told them who they believed in.

Faith gave them something and hope gave them some place, but love gave them someone.

In the journey of life, faith was the boat, hope the anchor, and love the rudder.

They had to maintain an ever-growing love for God and neighbor and they looked to Jesus to tell them how. One day Jesus told his apostles, "If anyone loves me, he will keep my word, and my Father will love him, and we shall come and make our home with him" (Jn 14:23).

The secret then was to keep his word and the Trinity would live in them. The Spirit made them sons of God at baptism; an indelible seal was placed upon them, never to be erased in time or eternity. Like the sons of men, they had to grow and mature in their new life and that life was fed by God himself.

"And my Word is not my own," Jesus said, "it is the Word of the One who sent me" (Jn 14:24). The "Word" was not only something they heard; it was someone they loved.

They knew that the words that passed through their minds and the emotions of their hearts were inseparable. In the scriptures, the sacred writers often used the word *mind* and *heart* as if they were the same.

Jesus himself told them that "whatever goes into a man from outside cannot make him unclean.... It is what comes out of a man that makes him unclean. For it is from within, from man's heart, that evil intentions emerge" (Mk 7:21, 15, 23). One would think that theft, murder, avarice, adultery, envy, and pride originate in the mind that reasons, plans, and determines goals, but Jesus says it all comes from the heart.

When we speak of the heart, we think of love; wherever there is love there is the possibility of hatred. What we love or hate determines our course in life, and the degree to which we love or hate will determine our success or failure.

One day Jesus said to a paralytic, "Courage, my child, your sins are forgiven" (Mt 9:2). The scribes were incensed that Jesus forgave sins. Because only God can forgive sins, their only thought was that Jesus was blaspheming. Scripture then gives us one of those instances where mind and heart are synonymous: "Knowing what was in their minds Jesus said, 'Why do you have such wicked thoughts in your hearts?'" (Mt 9:4-5). Jesus knew what they were thinking and yet he spoke of those invisible and inaudible words as coming from the heart.

"When anyone hears the word of the Kingdom without understanding, the evil one comes and carries off what was sown in his heart" (Mt 13:19). Here again Jesus speaks of the heart as a receptacle of knowledge, and yet we all realize that it is the mind, operating through the brain, that retains knowledge, reasons, and accomplishes.

Many scientists declare that a human being is legally dead when his brain stops functioning and others maintain he is dead when his heart stops. It is a problem that will be difficult to solve in both physical and spiritual realms. In scripture, however, Jesus joins the two together very often and seems to indicate that as the heart pumps blood to the brain to keep it functioning in the physical realm, the three faculties of the soul, operating through the mind, are also influenced.

The heart, the symbol of love and seat of the emotions, reaches out as a light shining in the world, indicating the power of our will and the direction we have chosen to take.

Hearts for the Kingdom

No matter how often we remember Jesus' words, or how deeply we believe in them, if those words do not affect our heart and move that heart to love and give all to Jesus, it is nothing. St. Paul realized this when he said to the Corinthians that if he had all knowledge, gave everything he possessed to the poor, gave his body to be burned, and had the faith that moved mountains, without love, it would be as nothing (1 Cor 13:1-3).

Paul was not speaking of an emotional love that was fanned into a raging blaze then quickly turned into ashes. No, he was speaking of a deep love of the heart, an inner conviction, a total consecration, a drive that preferred death to denial.

The heart of the Christian was a heart of flesh, penetrated by the Spirit of the Lord. It was a heart ever aware of being a "home" in which the Spirit of the Lord reigned and loved.

The disciples going to Emmaus had this experience when Jesus began to walk beside them. After they recognized him in the breaking of bread, they said to each other, "Did not our hearts burn within us as he talked to us on the road and explained the Scriptures to us?" (Lk 24:32).

Loving Jesus was a heart experience just as much as an intellectual acceptance of him as Lord and Savior. This is what gave these converts life and joy. They became lovers of God and faithful children, not only obedient subjects. They loved him and he loved them. They dwelt in him as he dwelt in them through the power of the Holy Spirit.

Jesus had assured them that "a good man draws what is good from the store of goodness in his heart. . . . For a man's words flow out of what fills his heart" (Lk 6:45). They were to be vigilant and not permit anything to enter the door of their souls that would destroy or mar its beauty. "Watch yourselves," he told them, "or your hearts will be coarsened with debauchery and drunkenness and the cares of life" (Lk 21:34).

Jesus puts the "cares of life" in the same category as debauchery and drunkenness. All three weaknesses occupy the mind and heart. The mind becomes possessed by them, the heart revels in them, and Jesus and the kingdom are pushed aside as something not relevant for the moment.

The first Christians never forgot the statement Jesus made one day when he said, "Store up treasures for yourself in heaven, where neither moth nor woodworms destroy them and thieves cannot break in and steal. For where your treasure is, there will your heart be also" (Mt 6:20, 21).

It was of primary importance then that they analyze their priorities to be sure the one thing necessary—the kingdom— was first and foremost. The first Christians' goal was to pattern their lives after the life of Jesus. They were sons of God through grace and they made sure that sin would not take that treasure away from them. However, their lives as Christians were more positive than negative. They not only safeguarded their treasure, they increased it every day by seizing every opportunity to grow into the likeness of Jesus. Their whole life was spent setting their hearts aright and changing those hearts to resemble Jesus.

The Heart of Jesus

"Shoulder my yoke and learn from me, for I am gentle and humble in heart, and you will find rest for your souls" (Mt 11:29-30). The Father had given each of them the yoke of obeying the commandments, and especially the new one—to love their neighbor as he loved them. Jesus took that yoke upon himself when he became man, and he bore it by being meek and humble of heart.

The first Christians were to learn how to preserve their hearts' treasure by doing as Jesus did always and everywhere. The realization that heaven existed detached them from the world; the words of Jesus gave them something to hang on to when the going was difficult. But they needed a heart united to the very heart of God to persevere in maintaining and increasing their treasure in heaven.

The heart of Jesus gave the souls of these Christians peace and rest. The apostles often related to them how, when Jesus appeared to them after the resurrection, he said, "Peace be with you! . . . Why are you so agitated, and why are these doubts rising in your hearts?" (Lk 24:36, 39).

Like the apostles before them, the first Christians had to fight doubt and fear many times but they would unite their hearts to his. They would love as he loved and have the same goal and determination as he.

He came as light and they would be the radiation of that light. He showed mankind the Father's love and they would be an example of that love. He was detached and never lost sight of his Father and they would be detached and never lose sight of him. As Jesus manifested the Father, they would manifest Jesus.

Jesus said he only did what he saw the Father do. The first Christians strove with all their power to do as Jesus did. "The proof," Paul told them, "that you are sons is that God has sent the Spirit of his Son into our hearts: the Spirit that cries, 'Abba, Father'" (Gal 4:6).

They were to be patient and persevere in being like Jesus. They were to be "happy, always happy in the Lord," full of that peace that guarded their hearts and thoughts in Christ Jesus (Phil 4:4,7). Their hearts were to belong to Jesus; he was their first love; he was the center of their day, their life, their work, their goals. He was truly the heart of their hearts and they safeguarded this treasure with determination and zeal.

They kept his words in their minds and his love in their hearts and together they changed their lives, "so that Christ may live in your hearts through faith, and then, planted in love and built in love," they would begin to understand the infinite love of God, as he gave them his very Spirit to dwell in their hearts (Eph 3:16-20).

Their lives were living witnesses of the love of Jesus. St. Paul told them, "You are a letter from Christ, drawn up by us and written not with ink but with the Spirit of the living God; not on stone tablets but on the tablets of your living hearts" (2 Cor 3:3).

THREE

Prayer in Anguish

THE FIRST CHRISTIANS experienced moments of ecstasy, hours of happiness, a perpetual joy, and deep anguish of heart. Life for them changed but the change for the better was within. Although their inner self was more important, their life in the world clamored for attention and often caused them their greatest pain.

It is always painful to change anything and perhaps the greatest pain of all is the loneliness of change. This was the first deep pain the Christians experienced. They suddenly stood alone in the world as strangers. Everything and everyone was different and many times opposed to their way of thinking and living.

Only a short time before, they were comfortable in the world; when Jesus entered their hearts they were cut off from that world and became as foreigners in a land of exile. Many times they had to recall the words of Jesus: "If the world hates you, remember that it hated me before you. . . . my choice withdrew you from the world. . . . [Father,] I am not asking you to remove them from the world, but to protect them from the Evil One" (Jn 15:18, 19; 17:15). The Christians had something glorious within them, something they talked about, shared, and struggled for, but they could not give it to anyone. It was a gift and that gift of faith spread by its manifestation in their lives.

Separation

It was a great trial for them to realize that the very love in their hearts created a separation from former friends and divided father from son and daughter from mother. They looked to Jesus and realized that his life, too, was a sign of contradiction. His very presence in a crowd divided it immediately into two groups, those who loved him and those who hated him.

Like Jesus, they prayed for their persecutors but their prayers were mixed with tears and sorrow. While their lips moved in pleas for mercy, their hearts burned within them with love for Jesus. They realized with Paul that nothing could come between them and Christ, even if they were worried or troubled or persecuted or lacking food and clothing. They were threatened and attacked but God would turn everything to their good because they loved him (Rom 8:31-39).

All the Christians were hounded as criminals and sought for as traitors. The anguish in their hearts, severe and crushing, became a prayer. They were suffering for the sake of Jesus' name; they cried out to him and depended upon him alone for strength and courage. Fear often gripped their souls to the point where they pleaded for deliverance, but they kept their eyes on Jesus.

Jesus had warned them this life of exile would not be easy and so they saw everything as an opportunity to raise their souls to God in heartfelt prayer. Prayer was to raise the mind and heart to God; as those anguished days passed on into weeks and then into years, they became stronger and more serene. Their trust was in Jesus and they had no preconceived ideas as to how he would plan and dispose of their lives.

These Christians never separated God from everyday life. He was the cause of their anguish; he was their consolation in pain; he was the love of their lives. They would offer to him their distress, as well as their joy, as a pleasing sacrifice.

When their souls were fearful, they united that fear with his in the garden of agony. When their persecutors made them leave home and land, they merely saw the opportunity to spread the good news in far-off places. They listened for and to the voice of the Spirit as he guided their lives to a fruitful conclusion.

There were many uncertainties in life but they were all turned into a prayer. Everything remained outside of them; the heartaches that resulted from the malice of other men made them more detached and dependent upon their Lord and teacher.

They realized that the road between finding Jesus and arriving home was long and arduous but his Spirit prayed in them when they did not know what to say; he guided them when they did not know the direction to take, and he loved in them when their hearts were cold and distraught. Everything was part of an eternal plan they lived out moment to moment and used to the best advantage.

They gave themselves entirely to the Holy Spirit. Paul voiced the sentiments of all the Christians when he said, "And now you see me a prisoner already in spirit: I am on my way to Jerusalem, but have no idea what will happen to me there, except that the Holy Spirit, in town after town, has made it clear enough that imprisonment and persecution await me" (Acts 20:22-23).

Paul had given himself to God so completely that he was like a prisoner to his Spirit, ever obedient to his will, ever ready to suffer or die for the sake of Jesus. Paul could see more and more hatred for himself and his cause in town after town and he realized his time to preach the good news was short.

The uncertainties that brought anguish to the hearts of these Christians also brought with them hope and joy. They had a cause, a goal, a hero, and anguish of mind was part of the price to pay. They did not become bitter with their lot for they knew they would possess their souls in patience.

Desolation and Trial

These Christians suffered not only from the alienation of friends, persecution, and loss of home and land, but some of them also had bodily illness and desolation. There is nothing more difficult than pain within oneself, whether that pain be physical, spiritual, or mental. Man can withstand great trials as long as those trials originate outside himself.

No matter how strong the battle we fight may be, as long as our health and our hope are preserved intact, we can withstand the onslaughts. In the Old Testament, Job withstood all the calamities that Satan visited upon him with patience, fortitude, and resignation, but when his body and soul were racked in pain, he cursed the day he was born (Jb 3:1).

The first Christians were soldiers in the army of Christ, but they were not exempt from the ills of the rest of society. The master had filled their souls with sanctifying grace, made them heirs to the kingdom, and placed the seal of his Spirit on their foreheads at baptism, but he did not exempt them from the consequences of original sin. Their lives on earth remained full of toil and sweat but were changed by the power of his Spirit through a joyful acceptance of their lot, a hope for something better to come, and a sense of purpose that no suffering could dissuade.

Paul himself mentions his own weaknesses and a disgusting disease, neither of which were taken from him, as far as the scriptures report. When he did implore the Lord to deliver him from "weaknesses, . . . insults, hardships, persecutions, and the agonies" he went through for the sake of Jesus, the Lord replied, "My power is at its best in weakness" (2 Cor 12:7-10).

This was one of the most important lessons the first Christians learned. Weakness, illness, frustration, tension, and anxiety were no longer enemies to their souls; they were now used to show forth the power of God in their lives. Jesus would not deliver them from trials; he would give them inner power to overcome those trials, to be joyful in the midst of them, and to turn them into merit for the kingdom to come. These frustrations would be turned into precious jewels in heaven.

They had the power of his Spirit within them and they never had to fear the vicissitudes of life. When they hid in the catacombs in order to break bread and worship, they did so with a sense of finality. Every night new converts joined their ranks as others were taken prisoner or martyred.

Some of them left for other places and preached the good news everywhere. The more they were persecuted, the more people joined their ranks and the more love poured out from them. Their way of life and their love was fed by sacrifice and persecution.

They were children of God and slaves to no one. They were free; although anxiety became part of their daily lives, it was no longer a burden but a test of their courage, confidence, and trust in Jesus. They learned how to cope with every situation and turn darkness into light, and anxiety into serenity.

Paul's Suffering

Paul gave them courage and light when he told them, "I know how to be poor and I know how to be rich too. I have been through my initiation and now I am ready for anything anywhere: full stomach or empty stomach, poverty or plenty. There is nothing I cannot master with the help of the One who gives me strength" (Phil 4:11, 12).

St. Paul's life seemed to be wrapped in anguish. He began his career as a determined persecutor ill at ease until every last Christian was in jail or slain. His conversion resulted in days of distress as he realized that his zeal was misplaced and Jesus was truly God and Lord.

For seventeen years he prayed and studied his new faith and then found himself still feared and under suspicion. Everywhere he traveled, he had to fear for his life. His enemies among his own were numerous and they often followed him to discredit everything he said.

His apostleship was constantly questioned by fellow Christians. He had to defend his right to that title by telling them that he was a true apostle, for he had seen the Lord and exhibited the power of his Spirit by mighty deeds.

Not only by his deeds did he have to prove he was an apostle but by his suffering for the faith. He worked harder, was in prison, flogged, beaten, and shipwrecked more often than anyone else (2 Cor 11:22-29).

He was in constant danger everywhere and from everything including "rivers and the open sea." Most of all, his "anxiety for all the churches" and his fear of error in their ranks forced him to warn the Christians over and over again. "Be on your guard," he told them, "I know quite well that when I have gone fierce wolves will invade you and will have no mercy on the flock" (Acts 20:28, 29).

Peter's Suffering

Peter, too, had his moments of anguish. His terrible fall ever made him wary of his own strength and forced him to depend entirely on the Lord Jesus. This man of repentance and compassion for his neighbors was forced one day to make an example of two people who tried to deceive the newly formed Christian community. Ananias and Sapphira were struck dead for lying to the Holy Spirit when Peter questioned the sale of their property.

He had to reprove Simon the magician for trying to buy power. "May your silver be lost forever, and you with it, for thinking that money could buy what God has given for nothing" (Acts 8:20). Though Peter spoke under the influence of the Spirit, these occasions were full of tension and anguish of heart. To see men selfish in the things of God causes untold distress in the hearts of those who have given their entire selves to his service. The wrath of the Pharisees and the numerous

Christians martyred by pagan emperors gave Peter great concern and compassion for all those who suffered for Jesus' name.

And then one day Peter had a vision that was to cause him many an anguished hour. He saw heaven open and a large sheet lowered that contained every possible sort of animal. He was told to eat and soon realized that God was about to change his lifestyle. Peter was told by this symbolic vision that the apostles were to preach and to baptize the Gentiles for Jesus came to save all men. The first convert was an Italian centurion named Cornelius, and although to us it seems of little consequence, it was not so for a pious Jew.

Peter always felt criticism keenly. After the conversion of Cornelius he received a deluge of reproofs from the apostles and the brethren in Judea. To pacify them, he had to explain his vision and the power of the Spirit manifested in these pagans.

Peter and the other apostles were faithful Israelites and entrenched in the Law. They loved Jesus and believed in his word, but Jesus had not told them what to do about pagans. Did not Jesus himself tell a Canaanite woman that he had been sent to the House of Israel and that it wasn't right to give the bread of children to dogs? (Mt 15:25-26).

The brethren's acceptance of his vision was temporary and Peter became more and more in doubt as to his course. This uncertainty caused him many anguished hours. He prayed and continued to associate with pagans and baptize them. And then one day the inevitable clash came when God's will became clear and Peter's prayer for light was answered.

To solve his dilemma, Peter began to compromise. James and his friends began to teach that pagans must first be Jews before they became Christians. They put pressure on Peter and he succumbed. "His custom had been to eat with the pagans, but after certain friends of James arrived he stopped doing this and kept away from them altogether for fear of the group that insisted on circumcision" (Gal 2:11-12).

Paul and Barnabas had a long argument with them. At this time Paul said, "When I saw they were not respecting the true meaning of the good news, I said to Cephas in front of everyone, 'In spite of being a Jew, you live like the pagans and not like the Jews, so you have no right to make pagans copy Jewish ways'" (Gal 2:14).

It is interesting at this point to observe the action of real Christians in a heated discussion. They all decided to go to Jerusalem and present the problem to a council of apostles and elders. It was in such an assembly that the Spirit would speak (Acts 15:2).

These men were dealing with a conflict that caused each side anguish of heart. Each felt he was doing God's will and adhered to his own opinion. The difference between them and ourselves is that they sought guidance, prayed, and were objective in their opinions. Though each side was strong in its opinions, they listened and had the humility of heart to change when God's will was manifested.

Men of prayer may have doubts but they never lose faith or confidence in the guiding hand of God in their lives. Though they were men of great discernment, the solutions to their problems did not always come quickly like a flash of light. They traveled ordinary ways and had to wait with patience and perseverance for God to show them the way.

Peter's vacillating temperament had manifested itself again, but unlike the incident in the courtyard when he denied his master, this time he listened, waited, and prayed. His weakness was still there but he learned how to cope with it. His heart had told him that Gentiles were not to become Jews, but his mind had given in to fear. He made no final decision until he knew the will of God.

After a long discussion, Peter stood up and told the community gathered in Jerusalem that they had no right to impose the old law on the pagans. God is no respecter of persons. He sent his Spirit to pagans as well as Jews. Peter's discourse was eloquent and so filled with the Holy Spirit that all were silent.

It was at this point that the real Christian status of these men was apparent. James, the man most opposed to Peter's and Paul's arguments, rose up and told all those present that it was not just to make a pagan follow Mosaic laws before he became a Christian.

The Spirit brought to the mind of James a passage from the prophet Amos where the Lord God said that pagans would be consecrated to his name (Acts 15:17). He then ruled that a letter be sent to the new Christians asking them merely to observe some dietary rules to keep them from pagan sacrifices.

The letter written to these early Christians was short, but it portrayed a quality of soul and faith unknown today. Strong-minded men had deep differences of opinion on an explosive subject but they prayed to God and listened to his Spirit in one another. They all suffered from the rift that occurred when their disagreements became more and more apparent. Their sincerity and determination to find God's will made them say to the Christians, "It has been decided by the Holy Spirit and by ourselves not to saddle you with any burden beyond these essentials" (Acts 15:28).

Anguish of heart did not make these men lose sight of the Holy Spirit. They found him in the midst of tribulations and distress and like Paul they could say, "I am quite content with my weaknesses, insults, hardships, persecution, and the agonies I go through for Christ's sake, for it is when I am weak that I am strong" (2 Cor 12:10).

FOUR

Prayer of Humility

THE PAGANS THAT PAUL CONVERTED were, for the most part, immoral renegades, the scum of humanity. They had reached a level of depravity known only to those who have been there. They had no concept of life after death or a loving God. Life was an endurance test and a challenge to see how much pleasure could be squeezed out of every miserable moment.

This was the atmosphere at Corinth when Paul went there to preach the good news. He performed so many miracles and wonders that people would vie with one another for a handkerchief or piece of his apron so the sick could be touched with his clothing and healed (Acts 19:11-12). As Paul told them about Jesus, they saw in him a power and a strength they had never seen before.

When they realized that God loved them enough to send his own Son to redeem them and his Spirit to make them heirs, they left their old ways and began to live saintly lives. They experienced great joy and peace—a peace they never dreamed possible. They were completely caught up in this new experience and this new way of life.

Peter, a man of experience, tried to warn them, "Be calm," he said, "but vigilant, because your enemy the devil is prowling round like a roaring lion, looking for someone to eat" (Pt 5:8-9). But many of them began to relax their vigilance and slowly, imperceptibly, they began to slide back to their former ways.

They were attacked on every side. Some began to doubt Paul's authenticity as an apostle; others slid back to immoral lives. False doctrines began to spread and the argument about the law of Moses almost rent the Christian community in two. They were looked upon as "nobodies" in the world, and the constant fear of death made some of the Christians waver in their new-found faith.

"If any one of you shall suffer for being a Christian," Peter told them, "then he is not to be ashamed of it; he should thank God that he has been called one" (1 Pt 4:16).

Prayer of Weakness

Peter and Paul both had learned the prayer of humility well. They became wanderers going from place to place, admired by a few and despised by the crowds. Neither of these men ever forgot their past weaknesses. Peter, the denier, and Paul, the persecutor, were well grounded in the truth that they could do nothing in themselves but all things in him.

Because both were acquainted with failure and could correct with gentleness, they were veritable pillars of strength to the new-born Christians. The Christians who were immersed in the consolations of their faith had the tendency to become proud of themselves and their strength.

Though they were forgiven much and enjoyed the peace of the truly repentant, they often found forgiving their neighbor a difficult task and had to be warned by the apostles of their erring ways. "Wrap yourselves in humility to be servants of each other, because God refuses the proud and will always favor the humble" (1 Pt 5:5).

When their first enthusiasm began to wear a little thin and the Lord called them to greater heights of prayer by the desert of dryness and uncertainty, they began to look at their old ways. They wondered if they could not revert to old practices and sins and still remain Christians. Was not total dedication to the faith a little unreal in their society? Thoughts like these ran through their minds. Some wavered, and some fell deeply into sin.

False apostles and false prophets taught their own doctrines and those Christians whose faith was on an emotional level were swayed to new gospels. "Any newcomer has only to proclaim a new Jesus, different from the one we preached, or . . . a new spirit, . . . or a new gospel, different from the one you have already accepted—and you welcome it with open arms. . . . These people are counterfeit apostles, they are dishonest workmen, disguised as apostles of Christ" (2 Cor 11:4, 14).

These were Christians who fell not only into doctrinal errors but also yielded to immorality, laziness, and pride. Paul had strong words to say about Christians who did not live their faith. "You should not associate with a brother Christian who is leading an immoral life, or is a usurer, or idolatrous, or a slanderer, or a drunkard, or is dishonest; you should not even eat a meal with people like that" (1 Cor 5:11).

Paul explained that he was speaking of fellow Christians, not pagans. Unbelievers did not have the example of Jesus to pattern their lives after. They did not have the Spirit dwelling within them. The pagan's sin might be hideous but not as monstrous as that of a Christian who had the light but preferred the darkness.

St. Paul was a man of strong convictions, but his own sufferings made him realistic and compassionate. "If one of you misbehaves," he said, "the more spiritual of you who set him right should do so in a spirit of gentleness, not forgetting that you may be tempted yourselves" (Gal 6:1).

Not everyone was to correct an erring brother—only the most spiritual, those who understood the spiritual life and the weaknesses of human nature. They were to do so in a spirit of humility, realizing they could also fall if it were not for the grace of God.

The temptations of the Enemy and the spirit of the world

that surrounded them sorely tried their poor souls. The only weapon they had was prayer—shared prayer and private prayer—and when they fell in spite of all their efforts they would not despair. They would use their weaknesses as tools to arrive at a deep sense of their unworthiness and the grandeur of God's perfections.

They did fall at times, they exhibited many imperfections, but these failures never discouraged them or made them despondent. They realized that God loved them not because they were good but because he was good and they needed him desperately.

St. John made them realize this truth when he said, "God's love for us was revealed when God sent into the world his only Son ... this is the love I mean: not our love for God, but God's love for us when he sent his Son to be the sacrifice that takes our sins away" (1 Jn 4:9, 10).

How different was this concept from that of the Pharisees. These men thought they had to be good first and then they deserved God's love in return. "I thank you, God, that I am not like the rest of men" said one of them in the Temple.

He did not realize in his pride that it was precisely in being like the rest of men that he was loved by God. It was God who took the initiative and had pity on sinners—sinners who struck their breasts and said, "God, be merciful to me" (Lk 18:13).

God's Choice

"We are to love, then, because he loved us first" (1 Jn 4:19). How true this was in the lives of the apostles and the first Christians. The prophets of old like Isaiah and Jeremiah were sanctified in their mothers' wombs, as was John the Baptist. Elijah and Elisha lived frugal and penitential lives in the desert in an effort to maintain a personal contact with God.

When Jesus came, however, he began by picking out imperfect, "uneducated laymen" (Acts 4:13) who constantly bickered about their place at table and in the kingdom—men ambitious for honor and glory with little comprehension of a spiritual life. One apostle was a despised tax collector and many were Galileans, whose speech betrayed their ignorance. The only respectable Judean was Judas, who turned traitor.

It was as if God were trying to prove from the very beginning that "He chose us; we did not choose him" (Jn 15:16). Even after Pentecost God continued this pattern by giving Saul the charism of seeing his light, hearing his voice, and being knocked to the ground—all while he was a sinner and persecutor.

God looked down upon poor sinners and placed into their hearts his own Spirit so they might look upon him as sons look upon their father. It was nothing they merited, nothing they deserved. It was all his goodness reaching down from his mighty throne and lifting up their nature to a state beyond their wildest dreams.

"We were still helpless when at his appointed moment Christ died for sinful men.... What proves that God loves us is that Christ died for us while we were still sinners" (Rom 5:6, 8). Paul wanted to impress upon his converts the depths and goodness of God's love for them. They had to realize that God loved them when they were in a state of rebellion against him.

Now that they were converted, changed, and made new by the Spirit of God, they had to manifest their sonship by bearing the fruit of humility. This humility was not a downgrading of their identity. It was a deep awareness of the depths of God's all-embracing, personal love for each one of them with all their weaknesses and frailties.

They were, in the mind of the world, most unlikely subjects for the love of an omnipotent God, and that was the beauty of it all. They were unlovable creatures on whom God's loving eyes looked with mercy and compassion.

When they were chosen by that love they were not wise, influential, or noble. It was to shame the wise that God chose what was foolish in the eyes of the world. They were common and contemptible as the world judges its children. This was their boast. To shame the strong, God chose the weak. To show up those who had everything, he chose those who had nothing. He did all this because he himself would be their wisdom and virtue and holiness and freedom (1 Cor 1:26-31).

He would live in them and the remembrance of their littleness would make his power more manifest, his love more gratuitous, and his grace more precious.

To the pagans, these Christians were a contradiction. It would be human and natural to despair at the sight of one's frailties, but they saw the opposite effect in Christians who rejoiced at their weaknesses. It would be human to want to do everything oneself, but the Christians found joy in the realization that they had no power and that the power of Jesus bore more fruit in them.

They were once slaves to sin and at times they had to engage in a fierce battle to retain their new-found freedom, but come what may they would use every precious moment of time and every situation as a stepping stone to the kingdom.

They followed the Lord with the same determination with which they had once followed a life of sin. "As once you put your bodies at the service of vice and immorality," St. Paul reminded them, "so now you must put them at the service of righteousness for your sanctification" (Rom 6:19).

There was in their nature a constant struggle for the freedom of a child of God. They were ever conscious of something in the depths of their souls that sought sin while another force, even deeper, cried out for goodness, virtue, and truth. It was a lonely battle waged between invisible forces.

The Quest for Holiness

Their hearts reached out for holiness and their minds loved the commandments of their Lord, but in spite of all this there was always an intangible, invisible something that made them do what they did not want to do. It was a habit of sin they had formed and that came back to them so quickly they often stood back in awe at their weakness.

"Though the will to do what is good is in me," St. Paul told them, "the performance is not, with the result that instead of doing the good things I want to do, I carry out the sinful things I do not want. When I act against my will, then, it is not my true self doing it, but sin which lives in me" (Rom 7:18-20).

Paul had to admit that this behavior seemed to be the rule in his life. "Every single time I want to do good, it is something evil that comes to hand," he told his converts (Rom 7:21). But with one thought and one stroke of his pen, Paul told the first Christians how to solve this dilemma and contradiction. "What a wretched man I am! Who will rescue me from this body doomed to death? Thanks be to God through Jesus Christ our Lord!" (Rom 7:24-25).

He tells them that our reasoning power and our will power are weak, but thanks to God, Jesus came into a body like ours in order to condemn sin. Now, he explained, they were to live by the Spirit, not by the body. Since the Spirit of God had made his home in them, they were to behave as he dictated and inspired (Rom 8:1-11).

They were to remember that they were dead to sin and were to live a life according to the Spirit, and it was only because of this spirit that they would be free and at peace. Unless the Spirit of Jesus possessed their souls, they would not belong to God because "everyone moved by the Spirit is a son of God," and this Spirit in them made them cry out "Abba, Father" (Rom 8:14,17).

The struggle within them became a prayer—the prayer of humility. They were to decrease and he was to increase. They were to live spiritual lives in the Spirit and give up the habit of sin in their bodies.

In their very weaknesses the Spirit would come and help them, for when they were weary in the struggle, he would express their pleas in a way that could never be put into words, and God, who knew their hearts and their desires, would know what they needed (Rom 8:26, 27).

The fight to let the Spirit rule was at times painful, disappointing, and heart-rending. There were battles they won and battles they lost, but slowly and imperceptibly they changed and bore fruit a hundredfold. The struggle for holiness bore the fruit of Jesus, for, like him, they were meek and humble of heart, ruled by his Spirit, called "sons of God," and visible images of their Lord on earth. His power was truly at its best in their weakness.

FIVE

The Prayer of Hope

H UMILITY IS A LIBERATING VIRTUE, for it takes away from the soul the burden of any injustice. It gives us the freedom to leave everything in God's hands and the contentment to be satisfied with his plan in our lives.

Humility is an exhilarating virtue that keeps us from discouragement at the sight of our frailties. It is coupled with hope in an indissoluble union and together they bring our souls to great heights of holiness.

The first Christians were not afraid to remember their past. Humility covered it like a blanket. Neither did they fear the future, for hope lit the way. They were assured the path would lead directly to God.

They knew that faith, love, and grace were gifts from God, and hope gave them the assurance that the invisible reality was their possession now. They had only to cooperate with these gifts and give the Spirit the freedom to work in their lives. The Father had given them the greatest gift of all—his Son—and he would not refuse them lesser gifts.

The first Christians possessed a tremendous sense of expectation for the glorious gifts reserved for them at the second coming and in heaven. Their hope gave them the enthusiasm to look forward to his coming with eagerness. Salvation meant the resurrection of the body, the fullness of the gifts of the Spirit, the inheritance of sons of God, the glory of the kingdom, and the eternal embrace of God, their Father.

They knew that in their lives they had already begun this glorious heritage by sharing the greatest gift of all—the Holy Spirit. Unlike the hope in the Old Testament, which was an expectation of something to come, the hope the first Christians possessed made their heaven begin here and now because they were the temples of the Spirit.

Their hope was secure because it was based on God himself, who gave them his Son. He invited them to come to him through Jesus. He manifested his love by giving his Son's life for their redemption and then releasing the power of his Spirit to fill their hearts. Their lives were full of the joy of realizing that some day their bodies would rise and Jesus would come again and show the whole world that he was Lord.

In order to appreciate the kind of hope these Christians possessed, we will look at its various aspects and see how it kept them in a spirit of prayer.

Expectant Hope

It is important to remember that the hope the first Christians possessed was based on a promise fulfilled. Unlike the hope of Abraham, who waited for something to come, they saw the promise of the Father made manifest in Jesus. The life of Jesus gave them concrete proof of what lay in store for them.

Because he was their hope fulfilled, they did not need to be men of desires but men of expectation. Although their eyes had not seen the glory to come, they did know the source of that glory—Jesus. They felt his presence in their souls. They saw his power manifested by great and marvelous works in his apostles.

His own Spirit spoke to them in the depths of their souls and guided their lives with a loving providence. They were like children looking to their Father for guidance, love, and protection, and his presence surrounded them with an abiding sense of expectant hope.

"Blessed be God the Father of our Lord Jesus Christ," St. Peter told them, "who, in his great mercy, has given us a new birth as his sons, by raising Jesus Christ from the dead, so that we have a sure hope and the promise of an inheritance that can never be spoilt or soiled, and never fade away, because it is kept for you in the heavens" (1 Pt 1:3-4).

"You did not see him," Peter told them, "yet you love him; and still without seeing him, you are already filled with a joy so glorious that it cannot be described, because you believe; and you are sure of the end to which your faith looks forward, that is, the salvation of your souls" (1 Pt 1:8-9).

The word "sure" describes what the apostle expected of the first Christians. Their hope was not a "waiting" hope, but a "sure" hope. It was faith that made them look forward, but hope made them sure, positive, and expectant of the possession of God in his glory.

These Christians looked forward to the second coming and to heaven with a greater enthusiasm than we do for feast days, jubilees, holidays, and Christmas. We look forward to the pleasure and joy of a feast that comes and goes, but they looked forward to that eternal banquet that would one day come but never go.

This hope in them was so great that it brought upon them persecution and distress. Paul told King Agrippa, "And now it is for my hope in the promise made by God to our ancestors that I am on trial.... for that hope, ... I am actually put on trial by Jews! Why does it seem incredible to you that God should raise the dead?" (Acts 26:7-8). "It is on account of the hope of Israel that I wear this chain" (Acts 28:20).

The resurrection of Jesus was the foundation of their hope. Because they were sons of God through grace, they too would rise from the grave. This realization took away the fear of death. Their souls would enjoy the beatific vision and then, on the last day, their mortal bodies would rise and be reunited in a glorious state forever.

It is difficult for most of us, who have been born and raised with the concept of eternal life, to fully realize what it meant to hear and believe this truth for the first time. Their souls would never die—only pass over from one mode of existence to another; they would never cease to be. What a thrill that truth must have been for these new Christians!

"Yes," Paul told the Roman governor, "there will be a resurrection of good men and bad men alike" (Acts 24:18). As he told the Thessalonians, "We believe that Jesus died and rose again, and that it will be the same for those who have died in Jesus: God will bring them with him" (1 Thes 4:14).

These Christians were so excited over the prospect of rising from the dead like Jesus did that they began to wonder what would happen if they were alive when Jesus came again. When would he come? Would it be soon? Maybe tomorrow?

St. Paul told them at the trumpet of God, the archangel would call out the command and Jesus would come down. All those who died in him would rise and those who were living at that time would "be taken up in the clouds together, with them, to meet the Lord in the air" (1 Thes 4:16).

These Christians were curious about time and place. Paul, like Jesus, told them not to expect to know "times and seasons" for "the Day of the Lord is going to come like a thief in the night" (1 Thes 5:1-2, 3).

They were to live "in the light" and not like those who had no faith and hope. God had enlightened their minds to know with a certainty that he would come again and like him, they would rise from the grave. Faith and love were their shield and hope their helmet. Their souls were to be united to Jesus in such an intimate way that it would make no difference whether they lived during that glorious coming or not (1 Thes 5:7-10).

Living with God was to be a "now" experience and they were to be ready at any time the Master would call. This time of waiting was to be filled with good works and interior change. It was not a time for idle waiting and speculation. They were to give courage to the apprehensive, take care for the weak, and be patient with everyone. Most of all, they were to "pray constantly" by being happy in the Lord, and giving thanks for every detail of their lives (1 Thes 5:12, 18).

Hope—Inheritance of the Saints

This hope made the Christians realize that salvation was possible and "possible for the whole human race" (Ti 2:12). This was their main work in life—the putting on of Jesus Christ by the imitation of his life. Hope gave them the realization that they were called to be holy just as much as Abraham, the prophets, Peter, and Paul.

They had a calling that was just as important as Abraham's, and like those specially chosen, they had to give up everything that did not lead them to God. They were a chosen people set aside and paid for by the blood of Jesus.

"He sacrificed himself," Paul reminded them, "in order to set us free from all wickedness and to purify a people so that it could be his very own and would have no ambition except to do good" (Ti 2:15).

It wasn't because of any good action on their part that he chose them. No, it was the compassion of the Father, the love of Jesus, and the power of his Spirit that brought them up from a life of slavery into a life of grace and made them brothers of the saints, heirs that looked forward to inheriting the land of their Father.

They were God's children and they looked upon this dignity with gratitude and humility. It was real to them and although they had not seen the glory of their home, they had hope that gave them a glimpse into that invisible realm. They would see God as he really was and that experience would place their souls and eventually their bodies in a state of joy that was inexpressible in human language.

Being children and heirs gave them an awareness of love they had never known before and it was fed by hope. That love reached out to their neighbor and made that neighbor also desire to belong to God's family. Hope made the word *chosen* mean something very special in their lives. It made them reach further, work harder, give up more and love much. It put joy on their faces, laughter on their lips, and a song in their hearts.

They possessed his Spirit, they were his temple, they would live and breathe by the Spirit and "be holy just as he is holy" (1 Jn 3:7).

Lest their hope degenerate into presumption, Paul warned them, "We must be content to hope that we shall be saved—our salvation is not in sight, we should not have to be hoping for it if it were—but, as I say, we must hope to be saved since we are not saved yet—it is something we must wait for with patience" (Rom 8:24, 25).

This was not a contradiction to his doctrine that we are saved by our faith in Jesus. He wanted his converts to understand that without a change of life, an adherence to his word, and a deep love for their neighbor, salvation would not be theirs.

The basis of their faith was that Jesus is Lord. He was sent by the Father, lived, died, and rose from the grave. Because he is the Lord, his life, sufferings, death, and resurrection merited for mankind the forgiveness of their sins and made them like him—sons of God. This had to go beyond the "knowledge" stage and affect their lives in a radical, dramatic way.

The knowledge of a historical Jesus was not enough, for the enemy possesses the knowledge that Jesus is Lord and he is not saved. It is his very belief and rejection of that knowledge that creates his hell. He will not accept Jesus as Lord in his life. His pride recoils at the realization that the Son of God assumed our human nature and became man. This knowledge and his rebellion against it is pride—the kind of pride that puts itself above the wisdom of God and says, "I will not serve" (Jer 2:20).

The mere knowledge or belief that Jesus is Lord is not sufficient for salvation. When Paul told the Christians that faith in Jesus saved them and John told them that whoever believed that Jesus is Lord is saved, they were encouraging a change of lifestyle. "Do not model yourselves on the behavior of the world around you," Paul told them, "but let your behavior change, modeled by your new mind. This is the only way to discover the will of God and know what is good, what it is that God wants, what is the perfect thing to do. . . . Do not let your love be a pretense, but sincerely prefer good to evil. . . . Do not allow yourselves to become self-satisfied" (Rom 12:2, 9, 16).

St. John made some startling statements in regard to his concept of what it means to believe in Jesus—the Jesus who saves. He told his converts that they were to be "pure as Christ." To live a holy life, he told them, "is to be holy as he is holy. . . . Anybody not living a holy life and not loving his brother is no child of God's. . . . our love is not to be just words or mere talk, but something real and active; only by this can we be certain that we are children of the truth" (1 Jn 3:3, 10, 18).

It is only through Jesus that we enter the kingdom, for he merited grace for our souls so we may see the face of our Father. This means we must be like him; in the measure our faith changes us, in that measure shall we be like him. Our belief in Jesus as Lord must affect the conduct of our lives or we shall be accused of being children of light and preferring darkness.

This is very evident in the lives of the apostles. They all began by believing that Jesus was the son of God, the expected one. Eleven of these men believed and changed, even though at times they fell through their weaknesses. But Judas rebelled against change in his life and that rebellion turned love into hatred—hatred that was not satisfied until the man he once loved was destroyed.

All twelve believed Jesus was the Messiah, but the belief of Judas stopped short at the need to change and he destroyed his Lord. For a moment, Peter's faith stopped short and he denied his Lord, but love triumphed and he repented. When Peter remembered that Jesus had foretold his denial he remembered his admonition, "Once you have recovered, you in your turn must strengthen your brothers" (Lk 22:32). Peter was to use his failure to further his determination to change his own life and to help others change their lives.

This does not mean that anything we do or become has the power to save us; it only means that we must cooperate with the Holy Spirit and his grace and inspirations.

God has given and chosen but we must accept and respond. His love is gratuitous and infinite and we must reciprocate with all the love we possess. He desires all men to be holy, to be saved; but he will not force us to be holy or to love him. It is a union of love and of wills that fills us with him and empties us of ourselves: he must increase and we must decrease. In the process we find our true selves—that self that he created to his image and likeness, that self that sin has disfigured and weakness disabled, that self that has been reborn and made glorious by the precious blood of Jesus.

Yes, these first Christians were under no illusions. They knew what God had done for them and what they were to do in return and together they formed a partnership that continued into eternity.

Hope of Eternal Glory

There was one aspect of hope that the first Christians learned quickly: the need to persevere. Jesus had told them one time that a man who began to build a house he could not finish would be laughed at by his neighbors (Lk 14:30).

The more they formed the habit of being like Jesus, the holier they became; the longer they persevered in this path, the greater became their hope. St. Paul told them, "We can boast about looking forward to God's glory. But that is not all we can boast about; we can boast about our sufferings. These sufferings bring patience, we know, and patience brings perseverance, and perseverance brings hope, and this hope is not deceptive, because the love of God has been poured into our hearts by the Holy Spirit" (Rom 5:2-5).

God himself, through his Holy Spirit, was the source of their hope. He it was who bore fruit in them—fruit that lasted. Jesus made this clear during the Last Supper discourse. "I commissioned you to go out and bear fruit," he said, "fruit that will last" (Jn 15:16).

Unlike the people of the world who are good one day and bad the next, the Christians, who bore within their souls the very Spirit of God, persevered in bearing fruit by the very stumbling block that made those of the world fall, that is, suffering.

Persecutions, hardships, and sickness were not occasions of discouragement and despair—they were occasions to imitate, to bear fruit, to rise above, and to exhibit joyful detachment. These things, cheerfully borne, made them patient. The less they "kicked against the goad," the more control they possessed of every situation.

They became less and less frantic at every disappointment because, like Jesus, they saw the Father's providence in everything. Life had a purpose and a goal and a challenge hidden within its very existence. They were not going to be like those who "beat the air." They would make every moment count for eternity and add to the glory of that heavenly place.

Selfishness was not the motive of their anticipating the glory to come. It was the joy of children, grateful to their Father for his beneficent providence, that made them look forward to what was to come. God himself would help them to use everything to that very end. St. Paul encouraged them in the way by saying, "We know that by turning everything to their good God co-operates with all those who love him, with all those that he has called according to his purpose. They are the ones he chose . . . to become true images of his Son. . . . those he called he justified and with those he justified, he shared his glory" (Rom 8:28-30). They would share in the very glory of God because Jesus came down and paved a way for them, marked it with his precious blood, and walked its path so they would follow in his footsteps.

Yes, Paul realized that "hope would make them cheerful"

because it was rooted in the one who would one day share his glory with them. On earth they were envoys of God, "letters from Christ" to the world—confident because the Spirit living within them would give their souls a brightness and a splendor beyond their wildest dreams (Rom 12:12; 2 Cor 3:3, 9).

When Moses went up the mountain to speak to God, his face shone with such splendor that the Israelites could not look upon him. What man ever read that account and did not desire that kind of holiness—so bright, so glorious, that it shone like the sun? Paul, however, tells his Christians that because of Jesus and the grace of the Spirit in them, the splendor of Moses is as nothing! "Compared with this greater splendor, the thing that used to have such splendor now seems to have none" (2 Cor 3:10-11).

When Paul describes the splendor of the soul of a Christian, one feels he is in the presence of God. He compares the brightness of Moses as something outside of him, a glory that spoke to the people like a charism. It manifested in a dramatic way that Moses had truly spoken to God.

The splendor of the Christian soul, however, was greater, for that very God dwelt in his soul and changed him into Jesus. As this splendor worked wonders, the Christians grew continually brighter. Paul could only describe it by saying, "We, with our unveiled faces reflecting like mirrors the brightness of the Lord, all grow brighter and brighter as we are turned into the image that we reflect; this is the work of the Lord who is Spirit" (2 Cor 3:18).

They were not only in his presence as Moses was, but that presence was within them and its power transformed them into Jesus—into sons of God—living mirrors of God. They had a sublime mission, "to radiate the light of the knowledge of God's glory, the glory on the face of Christ" (2 Cor 4:6).

Because "earthenware jars" held this treasure, they realized that this power to transform them came from God. The "inner man was renewed day by day," and there was a purpose in all their difficulties. "Yes," Paul told them, "the troubles which are soon over, though they weigh little, train us for the carrying of a weight of eternal glory which is out of all proportion to them" (2 Cor 4:16-17).

As Christians, they were to live in heaven all the way to heaven. Because they had died to the things of this world, they were to "look for the things that are in heaven, where Christ is, sitting at God's right hand." Paul reminded them, "Let your thoughts be on heavenly things, not on the things that are on earth," because "when Christ is revealed . . . you too will be revealed in all your glory with him" (Col 3:1, 4).

They were truly destined to share his glory and no one would ever take away that hope for it came from God and led them to God.

SIX

Prayer of Peace

THE WORD *peace* meant more to the first Christians than the absence of war. In fact, their very fruit in Jesus created conditions conducive to war. Evil men who saw in the Christians a spirit of holiness were determined to eradicate them from the face of the earth. Their hatred for Jesus and his followers engendered persecutions and perpetrated cruelties that were insane and inhuman.

These Christians were under no illusions that being a Christian made all men love them or assured them of a place in this world. They lived in an atmosphere of the worst kind of war—the war between consciences, between ideals and goals, and between spirits. Jesus made it clear that he was a God of peace but he would not bring peace. "Do not suppose," he said, "that I have come to bring peace to the earth: it is not peace I have come to bring, but a sword. For I have come to set a man against his father, a daughter against her mother, a daughter-in-law against her mother-in-law. A man's enemies will be those of his own household" (Mt 10:34-36).

The life Jesus required of his followers made dissension inevitable, for those requirements left no doubts and presented no alternatives. Every man from then on who had to make a choice would cause some kind of turmoil in the lives of others. The Son of God became man and showed us all how a child of God must live. With the force of his example behind his words, Jesus divided all mankind into two groups and gave to each individual a choice to make—either for him or against him.

His love, mercy, and salvation would be extended to all but he would never interfere with their free will. He offered peace to all but many would not accept it because the peace he offered was born from within—a peace that rose from the ashes of interior violence in the heart of man.

The refusal of some to accept peace on his terms caused Jesus to shed tears of anguish. Scripture tells us that "as he drew near and came in sight of the city he shed tears over it and said, " 'If you in your turn had only understood on this day the message of peace!' " (Luke 19:41-42).

It was not man-made peace that Jesus desired for his followers. That kind of peace was short-lived for it was dependent upon the will and gratification of the strong. It always entailed the good of some to the detriment of others. No, the peace that Jesus desired for his friends was a gift that was part of himself.

"Peace I bequeath you," he told them, "my own peace I give you, a peace the world cannot give, this is my gift to you" (Jn 14:27). The only kind of peace the world can give is to determine who among its inhabitants is the strongest and most influential, and then those who are weaker stand aside until they become strong and the whole process of war begins again. Greed and the desire for power is the seed that sprouts dissension and war. It is seldom that real injustice brings about a just war. The Christian had to root out of his soul all greed and worldly ambition. This is why the world was incapable of giving him peace, for the Christian removed from his soul both the cause of war and the false peace that comes from the absence of turmoil.

Jesus the Source of Peace

The source of peace for the Christian was and is Jesus. Jesus told his apostles that when they were scandalized in him and each went his own way, he would not be alone, for the Father was with him. Jesus had found his peace in the Father; because he was always united to the Father and saw the Father in every situation, he never lost his peace.

This was the secret of his peace: union with the Father. His peace was not of this world; to make this clear he said to them, "I have told you all this so you may find peace in me. In the world you will have trouble, but be brave: I have conquered the world" (Jn 16:33).

Jesus conquered the world by not permitting it to be the source of his peace. The world was not to determine when he had or did not have peace. His peace was a sure, ever-flowing river, coming to him from the Father. He wanted his followers to find their peace in him just as he found his peace in the Father.

St. Paul told the Romans that Christ came "to bring the good news of peace" (Eph 2:17) and that he was our means of reconciliation with the Father. These Christians were to do everything in their power "to preserve the unity of the Spirit by the peace that binds you together" (Eph 4:3).

To the writer of the Epistle to the Hebrews, peace was an important part of the Christian's life. "Always be wanting peace with all people," he told them, "and the holiness without which no one can see the Lord. Be careful that no one is deprived of the grace of God and that no root of bitterness should begin to grow and make trouble" (Heb 12:14-15).

Peace was the very foundation of the Christian life, for peace made them free of the rancor and bitterness that prevented them from loving their neighbor and deprived them of grace.

Peter explained to the Christians the need to seek peace when he said, "Remember: anyone who wants to have a happy life and to enjoy prosperity must banish malice from his tongue, deceitful conversation from his lips; he must never yield to evil but must practice good; he must seek peace and pursue it. Because the face of the Lord frowns on evil men but the eyes of the Lord are turned towards the virtuous" (1 Pt 3:10-12).

The basis of Christian peace was virtue, and since Jesus was the one who bore fruit of virtue in them, it was the peace of Jesus they possessed. Peace did not come easily; it was the fruit of the divine indwelling—the fruit of the Spirit of the Lord.

Peace was precious to the first Christians; they sought it not for itself but because it kept them open to receive the grace of Jesus into their souls and prepared them to enter the kingdom. "While you are waiting," Peter told them, "do your best to live lives without spot or stain so that he will find you at peace" (2 Pt 3:14).

Peace formed a part of every facet of their lives. Paul gave the Philippians a blueprint for peace and it began with joy. He told them that he wanted them to be "happy, always happy in the Lord." He wanted them to be tolerant and never to worry. Most of all he desired that when they needed anything they were to pray for it, "asking God for it with prayer and thanksgiving." It was in this attitude of mind that Paul promised them a wonderful effect from this childlike confidence. He told them, "That peace of God, which is so much greater than we can understand, will guard your hearts and your thoughts in Christ Jesus" (Phil 4:4-7).

We see then that joy in the Lord, tolerance without bitterness, freedom from worry, and confidence in the Father's providence would obtain for them that peace that acted as a guard over their thoughts and hearts.

With the groundwork accomplished, he advised them to "fill their minds with everything that is true, everything that is noble, everything that is good and pure and everything that may be thought virtuous or worthy of praise" (Phil 4:8).

The peace of the early Christian was a deep union with God as Father, Jesus as Lord, and the Spirit as sanctifier. He raised his mind to the Father and drank in the realization that this great God was truly his Father. He let the thought of the

Fatherhood of God penetrate his soul until it rested in it like a child in its mother's arms—secure and unafraid. Power to withstand the trials of life accompanied this realization, for "with God on our side, who can be against us?" (Rom 8:31).

The Christian entered into the Spirit of Jesus and let his gentleness penetrate his soul. He not only thought of Jesus, he "put on his mind." He let the gentle, merciful Jesus take over his life to the point where he thought like him and loved like him. He was not satisfied just to pray to Jesus, he let Jesus bear fruit in him by giving his entire life to him. The peaceful Jesus lived in him and he would eradicate everything in his life that prevented that peaceful, gentle Christ from radiating.

The Christian never tired of contemplating the mystery of his soul being a temple of the Holy Spirit. He was very much aware that that temple must not in any way be defiled. He would adorn it with the beauty of love, peace, joy, kindness, compassion, mercy and self-control. He would sweep it clean if the mud of sin ever marred its beauty, and most of all, the atmosphere surrounding that temple would be one of peace. No turbulence was allowed to make its home there.

When storms were inevitable, they closed the doors and windows of that temple—their minds and hearts—and stayed close to the guest of their souls, the Spirit of the Lord. They held their peace, for in that peace was a shield against the enemy.

When they feared the future, they entered into his providence and held their peace.

When they were angry and disappointed, they entered into his gentleness and held their peace.

When they suffered pain and persecution, they entered into his wisdom and held their peace.

When they sinned and felt abandoned, they entered into his mercy and held their peace.

When death loomed before them, they thought of his promises and held their peace.

Unshakable Peace

Their lives were to be so united to God's will that nothing would disturb their peace. Every time Jesus appeared to his apostles after the resurrection he greeted them with, "Peace be with you!" It was as if he were constantly reminding them of the gift he bequeathed to them. His resurrection was proof to them that he was truly God's Son and his promises were true; the hope he offered was sure; the faith he inspired was real. All this was to assure their peace for it came from him, the unchanging God, and nothing should disturb that peace.

The first time he appeared to his apostles he questioned the motives for their disturbed souls. "Why are you so agitated," he asked, "and why are these doubts rising in your hearts?" (Lk 24:38). Agitation and doubts destroyed their peace and their master asked, "Why?" If they really believed everything he told them, why were they disturbed?

We have sympathy for these apostles who witnessed such cruelties heaped upon their master. We understand their doubts when the one in whom they put their hopes was suddenly snatched away from them and all seemed lost. He had explained to them many times that it was necessary for him to suffer and die but that he would rise on the third day. He was grateful for the love they exhibited for his pain and sorrow, but he did not understand why they were not anxiously waiting for his resurrection.

If he rewarded them for visiting the sick, how much more would he reward them for being compassionate towards his Passion. Their compassion was not his complaint, rather that their sorrow was selfish. It was mixed with a loss of hope, with a realization that the worldly glory they thought was theirs was gone and that Jesus was not a military leader delivering them from tyranny. This kind of selfish sorrow completely obliterated from their minds the thought of his resurrection; as a result, doubts and agitation took away their peace.

It is the same with us as it was with the first Christians. We are human beings and we feel pain, sorrow, separation, and disappointment, but we cannot permit these trials to disturb our peace. Nothing must be permitted to take away our hope in his word, his promises and his resurrection. In him we possess our peace, in him is our hope, in him is our faith, and in him is our heart.

He expects us to have such faith that we can move the mountains of doubt that obstruct the view of his face.

He expects us to have such hope that no disappointment, heartache or pain discourages us.

He expects us to have such love that we desire nothing in this world but his holy will.

He wills us to have such peace that neither the Enemy, the world, nor our own selfish desires can disturb its presence in our souls.

Peace is a gift we must ever pursue and, once we have found it, hold it fast, for it is part of him. With him in us nothing is big enough, nothing is great enough, nothing is important enough for us to lose his presence.

Peace and presence go together. We may not feel his presence, but his pruning love will preserve our peace.

We may have sorrow, but his presence will hold fast our peace.

Men of the world may hate us, but his peace will prevent our souls from being warped by hatred.

We may be hungry, thirsty, without home or land, but his peace will shelter our souls from the cold of discontent and bitterness.

We may be angry over injustice, but his peace will give us patience to wait for his justice to prevail.

We may be fools in the eyes of the world, but his peace will make us stand tall and unafraid.

To those in the world, peace is the absence of war, the absence of failure, the absence of turmoil, the absence of pain, the absence of suffering, the absence of hunger and thirst, and the absence of injustice.

To those who know Jesus, peace is his presence in their souls when they fail, when they are in turmoil, when they suffer, when they are in pain, when they suffer injustice and when ambitious men make war upon them.

To the world, peace is an absence of disturbing things, but to Christians it is the presence of Jesus in their souls that raises them above things. This is another reason why the peace he offers cannot be given by the world for one form of peace is dependent upon a presence and another upon an absence. His presence and peace are gifts to us and we must hold on to those gifts. Nothing can be preferred to them and nothing disturb that union of mind and heart.

Peace was to the first Christians, and will be to the Christians in the last days, an abiding presence that makes them see God as Father, love when they are not loved in return, stand tall in persecution, discern the difference between good and evil, be detached from the things of the world, possess a spirit of prayer, and ever be aware of the divine indwelling.

It was this kind of peace that the first Christians wished to everyone when they said, "Peace be to you" and "Peace to this house."

"To you all, then, who are God's beloved . . . called to be saints, may God our Father and the Lord Jesus Christ send you grace and peace" (Rom 1:7).

SEVEN

That Secret Place

MANKIND SEEKS PEACE, and yet it escapes him as soon as he thinks he possesses it. We are impatient over our lack of patience, angry because we are not gentle, and proud of our humility. Our souls are harassed on every side by contradictions, dilemmas, and paradoxes. We seek God, and here, too, we fall short of the mark we set for ourselves.

Our whole being reaches out and seeks its creator. We want to see God and touch God. Our soul cries out, "Where are you, Lord?" and then, as the silence closes its arms around us, we hope that some day we shall hear his voice say, "Here I am."

Will the sound of that voice, and the touch of that hand be reserved for Heaven? Shall we wander as through a trackless waste ever seeking, but never finding? No, God manifests himself to each one of us in various ways, in strange places, and at diverse times. We struggle on to find a way, a method, a ladder—something that will finally lift us up from our torpor and lukewarmness, and send us on a way of continuous union with God.

Is there such a way? Can a housewife, a baker, a plumber, a doctor, a lawyer, or a student be a contemplative in a busy world? Can people "on the go" pray without ceasing and find an oasis to go to for refreshment in the heat of the day?

Yes, there must be a way, and it is probably so close and so simple that our complex minds and complicated methods miss it completely. Perhaps we are so busy with things and so conscious of ourselves that we hunt for something when in reality we need Someone.

We live in a world where we are called upon to be very much "aware" of everything. We are asked to be aware of people and their needs, of our nation and its needs, of the world and its needs, and of course we are all very much aware of ourselves and our individual needs.

But what about the needs of our souls and their distraught faculties? How do we quiet our memory and understanding when they are out of control? Where do we go and what do we do when our interior world seems to be going in five directions at the same time?

Pray in Secret

One day Jesus gave his disciples a new standard. They were to love their enemies, pray for persecutors, give to anyone who asked, and be gentle of heart. After giving them these rather difficult commands, he proceeded to tell them to do two things "in secret." He said, "When you give alms, your left hand must not know what your right is doing; your almsgiving must be in secret, and your Father who sees all that is done in secret will reward you" (Mt 6:3-4).

This is not difficult to understand. When we are generous just to be seen by men, we have already received our reward. The Lord is telling us to be generous in imitation of the Father and to please him, not ourselves. Though our generosity may be observed by others, this must never be the motive of our almsgiving.

The important part of this discourse is what follows. We were asked to give in secret, and now he tells us to *pray* in secret. The reason is the same. We must not pray in order to be seen by men or for the sake of being considered holy. What, exactly, does it mean to pray in secret? His words were, "When you pray, go to your private room and, when you have shut your door, pray to your Father who is in that *secret place,* and your Father who sees all that is done in secret will reward you" (Mt 6:6). He then gave us the Our Father, which is a conversation with God, praising him for his glory, and petitioning for all we need.

Where is this "private" room or closet? Surely, God is everywhere, and the psalmist tells us that if we go to the heavens he is there, and if we go to the nether world he is there (Ps 139:8). Where can we go that is secret—a place where only the Father and our souls abide—alone and unnoticed by anyone?

In every home there is a closet, and if we were to go into that closet and shut the door we would experience two things— darkness and silence, a kind of thunderous silence. We suddenly feel and know we are alone, and yet the silence into which we have put ourselves becomes a companion. We are very conscious of the silence. It is no longer an absence of noise, it is a surrounding presence.

The silence itself is not God, but it is a condition, an atmosphere in which we become very aware of an invisible reality—the presence of God. The silence turns aside the veil that hides his presence from our senses.

We notice that our spiritual faculties of memory and intellect are quieted. We are so aware of the silence that it calms our soul. It is as if all tension and trials were suddenly lifted, and we are able to breathe freely for a few moments.

If we were to turn on the light in the closet, the darkness would be gone and we would be aware of everything in the closet—clothes, hats, shoes, knickknacks, and other assorted "things," but the silence would remain—we would still be aware of the silence. We have then two ways of becoming aware of the silence in the closet—the first in darkness, and the second in the light.

Let us apply this principle to our souls. When we desire to commune with God to strengthen our souls for combat in the battles of life, we can close our eyes. When we have done that, we have closed the "doors" of our senses. We have for a few moments closed out the world around us. Now, like a closet, it is dark, and if we are quiet and become aware of the silence in our souls, we suddenly realize *he is there*.

Our will has determined to seek out its Creator, and for a few moments, in the quiet of that place, our memory and understanding are stilled and quieted, and we become aware of his silent presence. We can speak to him as a friend speaks to a friend; we can adore him as a creature does a Creator; we can love him as a spouse loves a husband; and we can praise him as the recipients of his beneficent goodness.

He is truly in this place, either by essence because his power sustains us, or by grace as his Spirit makes us sons of God. By entering into the closet of our souls, we enter into the darkness of his silent presence.

If we go into this secret place during the day, even for a few seconds, we will calm our emotions and begin to have a more childlike relationship with God. We will find in him a friend who listens, a Father who forgives, a spouse who loves, and a God who corrects and guides us.

When we begin to form the *habit* of going into this secret place to commune with God, we shall be able to continue being aware of Him when the lights go on.

When the lights went on in the closet, we found clothes and assorted knickknacks. Some of these things reminded us of the past whose memories are both good and bad. Some reminded us of the future and all the things we would like to do.

So it is with our souls. We may often close its doors (senses and faculties) and commune with God, but the lights must go on. We live with people and play a part in history. The world around us requires our attention, and often demands it, so we must learn how to keep united to Jesus no matter what state in life we find ourselves. No matter how much the world surrounds us, we cannot permit it to conquer us.

Jesus prayed for his apostles when he said, "Holy Father,... they belong to the world no more than I belong to the world. I am not asking you to remove them from the world, but to protect them from the evil one. They do not belong to the world any more than I belong to the world" (Jn 17:11, 14-15).

We are in the world, as Jesus was in the world, but he never lost sight of his mission, his Sonship, or his love for the Father. We, on the contrary, become very absorbed in the knickknacks in our closet. The clothes entice us; superfluities make us feel important; sophistication builds up our pride, and we forget why we were created, our mission, our adopted sonship, and God's love for us.

Our lives do not radiate our sonship because our eyes are blinded by the fifty-watt bulb in our closet. Our preoccupation with ourselves has prevented us from accomplishing the mission for which he prayed to the Father, "With me in them and you in me, may they be so completely one that the world will realize that it was you who sent me and that I have loved them as much as you loved me" (Jn 17:23).

What is Jesus telling us? He is saying that our union with the Trinity in our souls will make us so holy that the world will know that Jesus is the Lord. Our union with God must be patterned after the way the Father and Son are one in each other. This is how we will become holy and prove Christ's divinity. A Christian not only believes, he becomes one with his beliefs. His life must be not only good, it must be sanctified.

Christianity must be more than an adherence to a code; it must be a way of life, prayerful, serene, detached, unafraid, and strong. A Christian must be a living proof that God is alive, not by how much *he* accomplishes, but by how much God accomplishes in him.

Perhaps we can get a mind picture of what we should be if we think of ourselves as a large glass vessel, filled with the sand of our human nature. God desires that we be filled with the clear, transparent water of his grace, but we must empty our vessel of all the sand—frailties, weakness, and superfluities that keep the sand so hard and packed down.

Sometimes our stubborn wills rebel, and God permits our vessel to tip or fall, and then some of the sand falls out. Immediately, he sets it straight again, and begins to fill it with the water of his grace.

All during our life we empty our vessel of all those things that are not like God, and as soon as he sees an empty spot, he fills it with himself. Our vessels become more and more radiant with the beauty of God's love and glory, the more we empty ourselves and permit him to fill us to overflowing. Our neighbor can see God in us as in a mirror, and our vessel becomes lighter and more beautiful to behold.

Sometimes it becomes cloudy as the sand and the water seek to take possession, but when the battle is over and the remaining sand has settled, we notice there is an increase of water, and we thank God for the pain, the disturbance, and the suffering that gave us so much grace.

St. Paul reminded us of this when he said, "We are only the earthenware jars that hold this treasure, to make it clear that such an overwhelming power comes from God, and not from us" (2 Cor 4:7).

The object of our prayerlife is to empty ourselves and to be filled with the Trinity. The first thing Jesus did when he became man was to empty himself. "His state was divine, yet he did not cling to his equality with God but emptied himself to assume the condition of a slave, and became as men are; and being as all men are, he was humbler yet" (Phil 2:6-7).

Our mission in life, then, is to cooperate with God's grace, and empty ourselves, and be filled with the Trinity.

We are not to seek detachment to be free of responsibility, but to enable us to love both God and man with a pure love.

We are not to withdraw from the world to be alone, but to be with God.

We are to do penance, not because it erases our guilt, but because it wipes away the traces of sin.

We are to empty ourselves, not for the sake of self-control, but to be filled with God—transformed into Jesus.

There is no definite method by which we can become selfless. Each one of us has particular virtues and faults that make the process of becoming like Jesus different. We must look at Jesus, read his word in scripture, and ask his Spirit to enlighten our minds and give us that particular way by which we can best attain the goal he has set for us.

There are those whose personalities are complex, and their way of holiness is varied and changing.

There are those who are simple, and their way will be simple and direct.

There are those who will approach God through reason, philosophy, and intellectual probing.

There are those who will live their lives saying their prayers and offering their sufferings to God as reparation for their sins.

These and many other ways have two things in common: a desire to be like Jesus, and a deep awareness of his silent presence. The quest for holiness is difficult indeed without a continual growth in this awareness, and an earnest effort toward being like Jesus in everything we do. If we make this effort, we can have, by God's grace, the life of prayer the first Christians had.

Closing the Door

Perhaps the secret of all prayer and holiness of life is wrapped in God's plea to listen—to listen to his silent presence, that presence that penetrates our being and keeps us in existence, that presence that fills our souls with love and serenity, that presence that makes us strong when we feel weak.

We have forgotten how to pause—we want so much to keep going.

We have forgotten how to be still—we want so much to move on.

We have forgotten how to listen—we want so much to be heard.

No matter where we are or where we go, we can say as Jacob said, "Truly, Yahweh is in this place and I never knew it" (Gn 28:16).

He is not as far removed from us as we think, for we constantly walk in his presence, and he lives in the center of our souls through grace.

We listen to the silence of his presence in the quiet of the night, in the darkness of our souls, and in the hearts of our neighbors.

We hear the sound of his voice in the inaudible words that shout to us of his beauty in the flowers and trees.

His silent presence cries out to us when we see him suffer in the lonely and forsaken.

His silent presence asks for compassion in the downtrodden and the injured.

His presence, ever surrounding us like a cloak. warms our cold souls with quiet silence—comforting and reassuring.

He asks us to pause and understand his love, for, like his presence, it, too, is quiet and all-consuming.

His silent presence, like a bandage soaked in oil, heals the wounds of sin.

Our souls, like dry sponges, reach out for the water of eternal life, that they may be satiated with his silent presence.

We may lose contact with him, but he never loses contact with us.

If we are to live any kind of Christian life, we must be aware and present to each other, for when the sense of presence is gone, one of us is very lonely.

When friends become unaware of each other, they become strangers, and so it is with God. He stands at the door of our heart and seeks entrance, for he desires to abide there and rule as king.

He wishes to possess us, though he is never possessive. He

desires our heart, but only to fill it with love, so that we may, in turn, give more love to others. He desires our thoughts in order to raise them to the heights. He wants our whole being so he may raise it to his nature.

He wants very much to be at home in the recesses of our souls—a friend who is always there to console, to love, and to enjoy.

But the noisy world around us, and the distracted world within us, seem to unite in an effort to prevent us from ever arriving at a serene and continuous contact with God. However, we need these sounds and words to communicate, to learn, to teach, to understand, and to love.

Words are like magic, for they can change our moods and life almost instantly. Some words lift us up, and some cast us down. Some words anger us, and others calm us. Some words make us cry, while others make us laugh. Men have fought wars over words, and some have given their lives for God's word. Some words make men lustful, greedy, ambitious, and proud; other words make men repentant, humble, detached, and pure.

Some of the words that Jesus spoke divided father from son and mother from daughter. Some he spoke made prostitutes into saints and made thieves honest. His words forced men to choose between good and evil, but they also gave thirsty men the waters of eternal life. His words are always effective and grace-laden to all who listen with an earnest heart.

"Yes, as the rain and snow come down from the heavens and do not return without watering the earth, making it yield ... so the Word that goes from my mouth does not return to me empty, without carrying out my will and succeeding in what it was sent to do" (Is 55:10, 11).

The words Jesus has spoken have been fruitful for those who listened, but for those who shut their ears, his words have been ineffectual.

Words are those invisible sounds that mean so much, teach so much, and say so much. We are all afraid of ever being deprived of the ability to form or hear words, for then life would suddenly become a void, without dialogue—almost like the void over which God leaned and said, "Let there be light."

The Silence of God's Presence

Sounds are also a rich part of our daily life. The sound of music gladdens our hearts. The sound of church bells brings a moment of peace, and sometimes tears—when tolling the time of a funeral. The sound of a factory whistle means men are at work, and sirens tell us there is danger and make us fearful. Horns and congested traffic rattle nerves, and the ticking of a clock tells us how fast time and life pass us by. Automobiles, planes, and trains take us where we want to go, and the conversations of strangers make us feel lonely.

We are encompassed by words and surrounded with noise, and we cry out from the depths of our souls for silence, not the dead silence as in a void, or the silence that comes from an absence of noise, but the deep silence, that speaks inaudible words and vibrates with quiet sounds.

The silence we need is the kind that brings us face to face with God in an act of faith and love. We need to close our eyes and realize that the darkness we see is not an absence, but a presence—a presence hidden in the depths of our souls—a presence so close that all seems dark.

Sometimes we must be still and let our minds and hearts speak to him in words of love, praise, reparation, thanksgiving, and petition. And then, there are times when our hearts are full of grief, and we need only to sigh and be alone with his presence.

Sorrows and illness of every kind weigh us down, and then it is that we must go into our secret place, weary and pained, and enjoy the cool refreshing silence of his presence.

God is a spirit and converses with us in a quiet atmosphere because our minds are not capable of listening to his voice when they are filled with noise and confusion.

The prophet Elijah experienced this on Mount Horeb. "There came a mighty wind, so strong it tore the mountains and shattered the rocks before Yahweh. But Yahweh was not in the wind. After the wind came an earthquake. But Yahweh was not in the earthquake. After the earthquake came a fire. But Yahweh was not in the fire. And after the fire there came the sound of a gentle breeze. And when Elijah heard this, he covered his face with his cloak" (1 Kgs 19:11-13).

No man can see God in this life and live, because his glory would annihilate our poor, weak, human nature. The second Person of the Holy Trinity had to divest himself of his glory and become one of us in order for us to see God in this life. Now that he has conquered death and entered into his glory again, we live in his Spirit, and we must converse with him "in spirit and in truth" (Jn 4:23).

The beauty of his nature is like the fringe on the edge of his cloak; the mountains are like tassels scattered here and there as his presence passed by during creation. Everything created is a reflection, a shadow left behind, as his presence walks the earth.

Jesus himself spent many hours in the quiet of the night and the early morning dawn, communing with his Father. These are, perhaps, the most refreshing and beneficial hours of the day to listen to the silent presence of God in us and around us.

It may be a sacrifice for us to pray at these hours, but the strength of soul derived from even five minutes of such solitude cannot be measured.

We cannot give our total attention to God and the world together. When we pray, we are communing with our God and Father. We are attempting to praise someone who is beyond our comprehension, someone who is a spirit and invisible, someone whose being measures every breath we take and gives his blessing on each succeeding one.

Scripture says, "When peaceful silence lay over all, and night had run the half of her swift course, down from the heavens, from the royal throne, leapt your all-powerful Word" (Wis 18:14-15). God's eternal word, who was with him in the beginning and through whom all things come to be, chose the quiet of the night to give his first act of human praise to his Father. He was born into the world during the quiet of the night, and he shall be born in our hearts in the silence of his Father's presence within us and around us.

We are not often conscious of that presence because we do not listen to it. A blind person soon develops a consciousness of things he cannot see, and a deaf person develops a consciousness of sounds he cannot hear. These people do not suddenly acquire another sense to substitute for what they have lost. They merely develop what they already possessed. And so it is that a blind man senses the presence of a person in a room though he cannot see, and a deaf man senses a sound he cannot hear.

A blind person's hearing is enhanced to such an extent that he can almost hear a pin drop. A deaf person's sight is so enhanced that he can see beauty that no one else sees. All these things are accomplished because one who is handicapped utilizes other senses and finds new vistas to explore and new abilities to enjoy.

So it is with his silent presence. There are times when we must close the doors of some of our senses and faculties and concentrate on the one we need to find our hidden but ever-present God.

There are times when we must exert our sense of hearing, to hear God. We do this when we make an effort to be conscious of the silence within us and around us. It is in this way that we touch the essence of God, who is present everywhere. Where he is not, there is nothing—and so St. Paul tells us that "in him, we live and move and exist" (Acts 17:28).

We do not often think of moving in God, and yet it is true, for the psalmist says, "If I climb the heavens, you are there. . . . if I flew to the point of sunrise, or westward across the sea, your hand would still be guiding me" (Ps 139:8).

He lives in us through grace, but we also live in him through his essence, inasmuch as his omnipotence keeps us, and everything else that is, in existence. Our very being is upheld by him, and we need to be conscious of that silent power as it sustains us, rebuilds us, remolds us, and desires to transform us into Jesus.

We need to be quiet and let his presence penetrate our being by giving him our wills—and total selves. In the consciousness of the silence, we must raise our minds to the Trinity living in our souls.

We listen to the silent presence of the Father, and say, "Lord Father, beget Jesus in me."

We listen to the silent presence of the eternal Word, and say, "Lord Jesus, bear fruit in me."

We listen to the silent presence of the eternal Spirit, and say, "Lord Spirit, transform me into Jesus."

And then, when we have listened and become more conscious of their presence working the wonders of their grace, we can listen to that presence with our hearts, and say,

"Lord Father, I glorify thy majesty."
"Lord Jesus, I adore thy divinity."
"Lord Spirit, I praise thy sovereignty."

Our consciousness of his presence must not be negative or void. It must be ever moving, reaching, touching, searching, and attaining the Creator of our being, the Redeemer of our souls, and the love of our lives. We do not negate our faculties to find the absolute; we use them to become aware of our Father, Savior, and Lover.

We empty ourselves to be filled, not to be vacant. We reach within to touch God in the depths of our being, in the silent darkness of our interior. We divest ourselves of sight by closing our eyes and seeing him as Spirit and Lord. We close our ears to sound, that they may be conscious of his presence in the center of our souls. We speak to him from the depths of our sinner condition—poor and stripped of ourselves, waiting to be filled with his silent, healing presence.

Like a lone soul on a mountain top, we heed not the storm

below; we have eyes and ears only for the love of our hearts, as we wait in silence for him to speak and surround us with his warm, reassuring presence.

Like the gentle breeze wrapping around us, his presence begins to penetrate our being, and we know for certain that we stand before his presence—understood though we do not understand, loved though we feel unloving, in brilliant light though all we see is darkness.

It is like not having anything, and yet possessing all things; not knowing anything, yet being filled with light. God puts us in the cleft of the rock as he did Moses, as he passes before us and fills us with his presence (Ex 33:22).

Like Moses, our faces are turned toward the darkness of the rock, but only to protect us from his glory. His hand is always upon us, and when we leave our private room to face the world once more, we see his reflection in every leaf, flower, tree, and creature that walks the earth.

His silent presence has made our vision clearer for having been in darkness, our hearing sharper for having listened to the silence, and our hearts warmer for having been so close to his Spirit.

EIGHT

Looking at Creation

W ITH A LITTLE EFFORT, it soon becomes easy to listen for the silence of his presence within us, but these times of rejuvenation are few and far between.

Most of our daily lives are lived with the lights on in our private room, and it is difficult to keep our senses and spiritual faculties in control. If we concentrate on one of them, the others have a field day, and if we tackle all of them at one time, we become discouraged and distraught.

Our total person must be consecrated to God, no matter what our state in life. We have been commanded by God to love him with our *whole* heart, mind, soul, and strength—and we shall never be completely happy if we are found wanting in any of these categories.

When we speak of closing the doors of our private room, we speak of our five senses in particular. We are human, and everything must pass through one or more of these five doors in order to enter into the closet of our interior faculties of memory, understanding, and will.

We can acquire a habit of closing these doors during the time that we are alone with God, and, through practice, we can arrive at an unceasing spirit of prayer in the midst of the greatest activity; but until we arrive at this state of serenity, we must cope with these unruly senses that are capable of leading us to the heights or dashing us to the ground.

We must train them to work for us, and be careful we do not become their slaves. We must acquire a habit of using them to attain the goal we have set for ourselves—union with God. We must accustom ourselves to seeing, hearing, touching, tasting, and running "in the odor of his ointments."

Reflections of God

If we were to go to Italy and see the magnificent works of Michelangelo, we would be struck with awe and wonder. The works we saw would actually be what was once in the mind of a great man and a genius. Though the works themselves are not the man, they do reflect, in concrete form, the mind of the man.

And so it is with God. Every created thing is a reflection of God. It not only *was* in his mind, but it *is* in his mind at this moment. In fact, its existence is dependent upon its remaining in his mind. Every created thing that our senses behold or experience is a reflection of one of God's wonderful attributes, and a visible, concrete example of the beautiful mind of God.

Just as we can get lost in a painting and forget the artist, so our senses can become so involved in their own pleasure that they forget the author of their delight. They do not see the forest for the trees.

We must perseveringly train our senses and faculties to seek the hidden, silent presence of God in everything, that they may serve us well in our quest for holiness.

Of all the images and things we look upon, one wonders how much of it we really see?

Sometimes we have the feeling that we are on a fast train, and as we look out of the window, we see everything, and yet we see nothing. It's all there, and suddenly it's gone, as some other scene quickly takes its place. When we arrive at the end of our journey, we say the trip was enjoyable, but, in reality, we have no idea of the beauty we saw. We did not drink in any of the beauty that gladdens the heart.

We have traveled and we have seen, but we have no memory to recall, no scenes to enjoy, no beauty to admire. Somehow or other, we missed it all, and our bodies are tired for having traveled, and our spirits empty for want of food. We starve in the midst of plenty, and are spiritually bankrupt in the midst of riches.

We need to slow down and see his silent presence around us. We need to take time to observe the beauty of a sunrise and a sunset, in order to drink in the quiet power lighting up the world around us or casting shadows over everything and spreading a cloak of darkness to tuck nature in at night.

We need to look at the trees in spring quietly pushing forth their leaves to give us shade in the noonday sun. We need to stop and reach down to a violet nestled in the grass like a purple jewel, and see the beauty of God, who gives such color to hidden things.

We need to gaze at the horizon, far in the distance, and see the vastness of his silent presence that is so attainable and limitless at the same time. We need to see him crying out in our suffering brethren for relief and compassion.

Our eyes must see more than things; they must also see the hidden power that sustains these things, the reflection of his beauty, the beneficence of his providence, the mercy of his love, and the glory of his majesty.

If, after the storms of life, our eyes see only mud and never see stars, then we shall miss the wonder of living and the awe in life. We shall have spiritual cataracts, seeing only blurred images of undescribable things.

We shall cry out with Solomon, whose eyes had grown dim of spiritual insight, when he said, "All things are wearisome. No man can say that eyes have not had enough to see, ears their fill of hearing" (Eccl 1:8).

The things we see must not distract us from God, for they are only stepping-stones on our journey home, to raise our minds and hearts to him. Our greatest difficulty in life, however, is seeing Jesus in our neighbor, but here, too, we must see more than meets the eye. To see his silent presence in our neighbor—no matter who he is or what he does—and to act accordingly, is the most purifying penance and the most rewarding experience. It gives glory to God and radiates the life of Jesus on earth.

We should understand that we must ever seek God and use everything to raise us to him. We speak of God being in everything—and he is—but we must realize that he transcends everything we see. A flower reminds us of his beauty, the smile of a child—his sweetness, and both are reflections of his spiritual, silent presence.

When we cease to seek God in everything, our souls enter a desert, and his presence seems to disappear. His presence is written upon everything, and as we read all the words he addresses to us in his creation, our reason begins to understand his existence and awesome presence.

Our spirit must reach out to his Spirit, as everything we see manifests his love, his providence, his mercy, and his compassion.

The works of his hands, so pleasing to behold, must never hold us prisoners, for they are mere reminders and stepping stones that keep his silent presence ever before our minds. On the days when our eyes see only the things of this world, the days we are so involved, the days that cares and worries hold us tight in their grasp—on those days, our souls feel empty and alone, for we have lost contact with his spiritual presence.

His silent presence in everything must raise our hearts to his utter transcendence. Everything in life is like a sign he left behind, a guide, a living message of his love. It does not say, "I am he"; it only says, "He is here." It does not say, "I am God"; it only says, "God made me." It does not say, "Rest in me"; it only says, "Let me raise you to him."

Every moment of life must be used to raise ourselves to God, who is above and beyond all his creation, and yet stoops to live in our souls through grace.

All creation is like a dewdrop on the tip of his finger; it

glistens for having come from him, but he flicks it down to us so we may see its beauty and say, "Oh, show me where you come from."

We cannot turn God on and off like a light bulb. He is the light of our lives and the source of our being. Our souls must ever seek his face and beauty in nature, his intelligence in man, his wisdom in our sufferings, his providence in our daily life, his omnipotence in the cosmos, his presence in our souls, and his essence in all created things.

Nothing should separate us from him, for our minds and hearts must seek him every moment of our lives. All of life is an adventure in seeking him out, and when we find him, his infinity gives us new vistas to explore and a greater capacity to fill.

Each day is new and glorious, for each day opens up to us whole new concepts to try and explorations to make. Each moment his silent presence hides itself, that we may seek and find him. Each cross hides his shadow, that we may take up that cross with a purer love. His heart rejoices as we go through life seeking him in every cranny and nook, reaching for his hand, and touching his garment.

Our eyes and ears must be open and ready to see him in every life situation. It is possible to see and yet be blind, and to hear and be deaf. When Jesus spoke to the Pharisees one day, he said, "You will listen, and listen again, but not understand; see, and see again, but not perceive. For the heart of this nation has grown coarse, their ears are dull of hearing, and they have shut their eyes, for fear they should see with their eyes, hear with their ears, understand with their heart, and be converted and be healed by me" (Mt 13:14).

The pleasures of this world can so dull our senses that they no longer seek or see God anywhere. We are afraid that if our senses begin to see and hear God, we will have to give up the multitude of trinkets we have amassed for ourselves. Like children, we cling to the toys that glitter and amuse us, and never grow up to see the invisible reality behind all real things.

When we limit God to the passing things of this world, he soon passes with them, for the limitless one cannot be limited, the infinite cannot be finite, the spiritual cannot be mundane, omnipotence cannot be powerless, and love cannot be constrained.

If we find God only in the springtime of life, when the grass is green and the flowers beautiful to behold, what shall we do in the fall when everything that was once so beautiful slowly fades before our eyes? And then, where shall we look when winter comes and the nights are cold and lonely?

A Christian is one who lives in an atmosphere of prayer and communion with God. He does not, and cannot *say* prayers without ceasing, but he does *pray* without ceasing. He makes no distinction between the spring or winter of life, for his soul ever reaches out, seeking, and sometimes straining, to see God every moment.

To some, the desire to be continually united to God in an attitude of prayer is impracticable, impossible, and improbable. And yet we admire a doctor who is totally dedicated to his work, a scientist who eats and drinks his desire to discover a remedy for cancer, a social worker on fire for justice, a man whose only goal is to become a millionaire, and a politician who spends all his time, effort, and money in the hope of getting elected to a public office. We can well understand how men can become absorbed in these pursuits, but not in the pursuit of God.

The first thought that crosses our minds at the prospect of always seeking God is that this effort will cause tension, nerves, and other disturbances. It is hardly in the realm of common sense to think that the God of serenity brings tension and the world of tension brings serenity, or that the God of love brings selfishness and the world of "dog eat dog" brings generosity. The tension in our lives does not exist from our seeking God, but from our effort to pursue the things of this world and God together, and from seeking to be filled with God, but not emptied of ourselves.

Raising Our Eyes to God

The first chapter of Genesis tells us that after God created the world he looked at it and saw that it "was good." If this is so, why the opposition between the world and God? Are we expected to wage a war on everything and everyone in the world in hopes of rising above to some supernatural state? The opposition does not come from the world that God created, but from what man has done with that world.

Instead of using it as a constant reminder of divinity, we use it as a resting place for humanity.

Instead of rising above the created to the uncreated, we sink beneath the created and find depravity.

Instead of looking at the beginning of each day as a gift from God, we rebel at the challenge and the sacrifice.

We do not understand why we cannot be totally selfish and full of God at the same time. We look at God as if he deliberately put us in a difficult position to test our stamina, and then, in our arrogance, we say, "It's all your fault. You made me with weaknesses, and then put me in the path of temptations, in a world of beauty and pleasure."

How pride has deluded us! He made us strong, but we made ourselves weak. He redeemed us by becoming weak himself, but we want to be strong enough to live without him. He wants us to set our hearts on the next life, but we want to stay on in this one. He wants us to die that we may live, but we want to live and never die.

He came and suffered so we would see the weaknesses we brought upon ourselves in a new light, but we think suffering in any form is cruel, useless, and sheer nonsense.

Our battle is not with the beautiful world he gave us to live in; it is with ourselves. The opposition is not from things, but from our *reaction* to things. It is our attitude, our goals, our desires, and our love that we put either in God or in ourselves.

The world and everyone in it can lead us to great holiness of life if we *will* it to do so. If not, it will fill us with selfishness and pride. Since the world can be used or misused, then, in itself, it is not opposed to God; it depends on how we use it.

A neighbor's hatred affords us an opportunity to be either hateful or gentle in return. The problem, then, is not in our neighbor, but in our *reaction* to that neighbor.

St. Paul says, "We know that by turning everything to their good God co-operates with all those who love him" (Rom 8:28). We do not often think of God cooperating with us, but our relationship with God is personal, and together we must use everything to help us towards our goal of being perfect sons of a perfect Father.

"Nothing," Paul says, "can come between us and the love of Christ, even if we are troubled or worried, or being persecuted, or lacking food or clothes, or being threatened, or even attacked" (Rom 8:35).

This great apostle had experienced all these hardships, and he realized that his reaction to them depended upon the thing he sought most in life—the love of Christ.

The core of our problem is in what we *seek*. If all we seek in life is perfect health, then we shall fear ill health, and this fear will occupy our minds constantly.

If all we seek in life is riches, then we shall abhor poverty or privation of any kind. Our thrust will be towards the possession of things so we never have to do without. We will fill our lives with fears and frustrations, as we forever seek the things that elude us.

If all we seek in life is glory, then we shall consider any humiliation as an evil and an injustice. We seek a soap bubble that perishes as quickly as a breath. We are so frantic for applause and praise that we seek only one thing, at any cost—the approval of men.

If all we seek is success, then the lessons to be learned from failure will be lost forever, as we become bitter with the world and everyone in it.

If all we seek in our neighbor is perfection, then we shall be scandalized and disheartened at his failures.

When we seek only the things of this world, then we are frustrated and disappointed at their temporal nature, short-lived pleasure, and the vacuum they create in our souls.

Our souls cry out to God to deliver us from our lukewarmness and torpidity. We reach for that invisible hand to hold tight to as we grope in the darkness, forever falling and rising in our efforts to move forward. Down deep in our innermost hearts, we know that only Jesus can fill us to overflowing—if only we could tear ourselves away from all the unnecessary pursuits that do nothing but weary our souls to death.

We want desperately to break away from ourselves and our selfishness, and belong to him completely, entirely, and totally—and yet, each day seems more barren than the last, and our efforts without fruit.

It is when we feel so useless and weak that we can take heart, for we know for certain that we *do* seek the Lord, or else we would find joy in this world rather than bitterness.

St. Paul had gone to the depths of his misery when he said, "For I am certain of this: neither death nor life, no angel, no prince, nothing that exists, nothing still to come, not any power, or height or depth, nor any created thing, can come between us and the love of God made visible in Christ Jesus our Lord" (Rom 8:38, 39).

He learned to seek God in everything that happened to him. He no longer sought God in good things alone. He saw God's wisdom in his weaknesses, persecutions, hunger, and even worry. He used every moment and every breath to see Jesus and be Jesus.

We, on the other hand, separate God into parts in our daily lives. We see him in some things and in some people, but not in everything and everyone. As a result, we think of him and love him sometimes, and then put him aside at other times. Our entire lives can be lived in a kind of "He loves me, He loves me not" attitude.

We are in St. Paul's third heaven one day, and down into the nether world the next. Some days we are positive we finally have found the secret of serenity, and then some unexpected and trivial thing comes along and we fail miserably.

But here, too, at least we *know* we failed, we *know* we have not come up to his expectations, we *know* we still have a long way to go. Yes, we have made progress while our pride was crushed and our feelings tempered; we are learning, painfully and slowly, to depend on him, the only source of holiness and strength.

We are learning to trust him because he hovers over us, guiding our path, wiping away our tears, hearing our sighs, and strewing little joys to lighten our burdens.

He is training our rebellious souls to listen to his silent presence, as we realize more each day how much we need him. We run to him, like soldiers after a battle, for refreshment and solace, and we realize that he was at our side all the time. We become so intent on "fighting the good fight" that we lose sight of the ground we have traveled and the gains we have made with his strength and his guidance.

This is the time we gather more courage for future battles—a time we take stock of losses and plan other strategies to conquer the enemy. Then it is we realize that our greatest victories were the times we stayed close, listened hard, and looked deep into his silent presence, hidden in every jeweled moment of our lives.

The other things we did to stay close to him brought moderate success, but it was the awareness of his presence, strong and serene, that raised us above life's petty crosses and gave us strength to carry the big crosses with calm acceptance.

It is a humbling reality to know that we can do nothing without him, and a hopeful experience to know we can do everything with him.

His Silent Power

The creation narrative in the book of Genesis is a beautiful example of his silent presence and secret ways.

When man invents or produces anything of any value,

volumes are written on the subject. But the sacred writer, inspired by the Spirit who hovered over the waters, simply and quietly states the whole of creation in less than two pages.

Some like to imagine the creation of the universe as some chaotic explosion, and yet our daily experience of God's continuing creation is to the contrary.

Every spring we witness a show of fantastic energy as each blade of grass, each leaf, each flower and vine push their way through earth, reaching for the sun, for color and life—all in silence.

We look at a fertile egg, warmed with a little heat, and in the silence of the shell, without the aid of any human intelligence, feathers, bones, beak, and eyes take form. And then, as if some invisible, quiet power tapped gently on the egg, a crack appears and a small, wet chick emerges out of the darkness into the light, to play its role in its Creator's world—all in silence.

Man prides himself on his inventions and computers that occupy so much space in noisy rooms and offices, and yet, the human mind, with much more than a memory bank, is so silent that no one but God hears it reason and decide a course of action.

Great generators operate day and night to produce enough electricity to light a few cities, and yet each morning the world lights up at the crack of dawn as the sun rises in golden splendor—in beautiful silence.

The rays of the sun, that so gently paint one flower red and another blue, draw up rivers of water to irrigate a bleak desert miles away—in quiet silence.

Man produces furniture, machinery, clothing, and food in noise, pollution, and confusion, but God creates a man in the small, dark, water-filled chamber of a mother's womb, with intricate physical and mental faculties that live and breathe—in powerful, creative silence.

Man invents large, bulky, clicking cameras to capture scenes of beauty. But the human eye, without sound, envelops whole landscapes, that imprint themselves upon the memory to be recalled at will—all in silence.

Man uses noisy televisions and radios, and the written word, to convey news of tragedy and evil, but each man has within him a conscience that reacts immediately to good and evil—in silence.

The machines that man invents to accomplish the work he cannot do are heavy, large, and noisy, but the nerve cells in man's brain, that originate those machines, are negligible in weight, microscopic in size—and absolutely silent in operation.

Men produce pumps and motors, attached to miles of electrical wires, to keep water moving from one place to another, and yet the human heart, created from a speck of protoplasm, pumps gallons of blood a day through miles of veins and capillaries, for sometimes ninety years—in silence.

Man produces energy in his other big machines, but he restores his own energy by quiet sleep. It is, then, when his machines are closed down that he can hear the silent presence of his God, in the darkness of the night and in the light of dawn. Somehow, he must rediscover that silent presence in between the noises of his new day.

When man initiates any kind of change, he does so with great fanfare and confusion, but infinite love initiates and accomplishes the transformation of finite human beings into sons of God through grace—in powerful silence.

If we spin anything around, or move a gear to turn a motor, it is done with great effort and noise, but God has the earth and planets spinning, revolving, and moving forward at fantastic speeds—in silence.

Men write, and noisy presses print volumes, explaining the scriptures, and then, one day, God speaks to our souls in a flash of light that opens up to us the most difficult passages—in calm silence.

When men give gifts, they are sure that those gifts are seen and appreciated, but God often bestows favors upon us that we are unaware of, because he does so in unassuming silence.

When men provide for us, they count time and money and all the effort involved; but God cares for us, guides us, watches over us, protects us, and inspires us—all in loving silence.

Everything our body does entails motion and noise of some kind—but the soul that directs those actions is as silent as the Creator who breathed it forth.

We are creatures of sound and noise, and we find it difficult to communicate with and in silence. But God works silently: his grace is silent and imperceptible; his sustaining power is silent; his providence is silent; his daily miracles of creation are silent; his mighty hand, as it guides nations and men, is silent; and his presence surrounding us, like the air we breathe, is silent.

It follows, then, that since we, as creatures, are noisy, and he, as God, is silent, we must communicate on his level, in his way, in his light, as intelligent human beings. It is in our soul that we resemble him, so it must be in the soul that our union with God, as Spirit, is accomplished.

Our lives resemble a search, a hunt for the pearl of great price, and all our thoughts and actions must be geared towards the finding of the treasure we seek.

NINE

His Purifying Silence

I T IS A PHENOMENON of our human nature that we do not see the things that are so much a part of us.

So it is that as we gaze at a beautiful painting, we are not conscious of the organ by which we see the painting. When we hear beautiful music, we become so absorbed in the enchanting melody that we are not conscious of the organ by which we hear. And so it is with the other senses. They are so close to us, and so much a part of our nature, that we lose sight of them.

And then one day when one of those senses is impaired it occupies our complete attention. If our hearing is suddenly gone or diminished, all we can think of is hearing, and we find no rest until everything is done to bring back what we have lost.

Occasions such as this make us both aware and grateful to the continuing silent goodness of God for the gift of our senses. How sad it is that we must first lose something to realize we possess it! How calloused and proud we have become to take his care for granted!

The physical abilities that we possess are so much a part of the whole person that we forget their individual character—and so it is with his silent presence. It is so much a part of our very existence that we are not aware of our possession of it. We think we are a totally independent, self-contained, and self-sustained individual. We lose sight of the reality of our complete dependence upon his love and power.

Although it is impossible to lose the presence of God, which is everywhere, we can and do lose the sense of his presence, and the results are the same as if we lost the use of a physical sense. We suddenly realize that we had something very precious, and now it is gone. Our souls feel lost, our feelings dried up, and our spirit parched for the fountain of living water. We stumble through an invisible maze of confused wanderings—searching, grasping, reaching, and groping for the hand that is not within reach, the face that is not in sight, and the voice that is as silent as the emptiness in our souls.

Why Dryness?

There are many reasons for this state of soul. For some, whose union with God is great, it is the very light in which they move so freely that often blinds them, in order to purify whatever of self remains.

For some, it is a purification of their love, that they may seek God for himself, know him as he is—pure Spirit—and love as he loves. For others, it is a purification of their hope, that they may put all their trust in him, understand their own weaknesses, depend upon his strength, and begin to possess him here as they will in the kingdom. For some, it is a purification of their faith, that they may believe though they do not understand, accept though they have nothing tangible to grasp, and live according to the word and revelations of Jesus, because they believe in his Sonship.

For others, it is a call to repentance rather than a purification—a call to return to their Father's house and regain the place they have lost. It is an emptiness to be filled, rather than a capacity to enlarge, for they have driven away their Lord by sin, and He seeks them out by the purifying sound of his silent voice in the depths of their conscience.

Regardless of what category we are in, or think we are in, the sense of loss we call "dryness" is always purifying, always a source of light, a closer bond of union, an opportunity for merit, a sign of love, an example of hope, and a manifestation of a deep faith. Every Christian who strives for holiness of life experiences dryness of soul. It is to most people a heart-rending experience. It is a paradox, for the soul becomes confused when it realizes that the harder it strives, the further away Jesus seems to be.

How strange is a spiritual life that draws a soul to a fire only to make it feel freezing cold! It is, to all appearances, a contradiction. In the world, the closer we are to a friend or loved one the more secure and unafraid we become. The deeper the love, the more glowing one feels in the presence of the beloved. And so it is as we grow in the love of God. He wants us to love him "in spirit and in truth" and this kind of love is above human love—as much above as is the difference between the flicker of a match and the noonday sun.

Human love in all its beauty and warmth must be raised to a level above itself. The air at the foot of a high mountain is easier to breathe, even though it is not as pure as the air on the summit. To breathe that pure air our bodies would have to adapt themselves to the atmosphere of the mountain peak. The peace and quiet and the view from that height are well worth the effort and the pain of climbing.

We would, however, encounter one phenomenon during our climb, a certain kind of loneliness. The further up the mountain we travel, the fewer companions we have. There comes a time when all things seem to drop behind and we find ourselves alone. When we finally arrive on the top, the loneliness is gone for we see things very differently. We see all our former companions and possessions as they really are with no illusions, no regrets, and no attachments. In this rare air of God's love we possess Wisdom, which is the Word of God— Jesus. We see things as he sees them because the breath of his Spirit fills our souls to overflowing.

To those who live in the sunshine of the valley, our life atop the mountain is forever dull and lonely only because they do not share the view. Sometimes we come down the mountain and bask in the sunshine, but soon we must ascend again and fill our souls with the fresh air of his love.

This is but a faint picture of dryness of soul and the beautiful work it accomplishes. There are times in life when God seems very close. The sun of his love shines brightly. Our hearts exult and our being is rapt in the joy of his presence. There are other times, however, when his presence fades away like a morning mist and we find ourselves shivering from the cold. If the whole world were to love and applaud us it would all be as nothing, for the sunshine of our life—God—seems gone, and our soul cannot be consoled except by him.

We wander from place to place looking for him, we try to pray, to meditate on his life, to imitate his virtues, but nothing seems to alleviate the emptiness in the depths of our being. Our life goes on and we work, eat, sleep, laugh, and cry but none of these functions fill the void.

There is a longing for God that does not seem to be satisfied by anything or anyone. A darkness descends but in it we do not sleep or feel refreshed. It is a darkness that keeps us ever awake—ever looking, ever yearning for the dawn.

It is a thirst that is never quenched, for every drop of "living water" makes us thirst for more. Days, months, and years can be spent in this state of dryness. Sometimes doubts as to the very existence of God surround the soul with their icy embrace and the blackest midnight descends and fills the soul with emptiness.

Though our poor human nature rebels at this state of soul, it realizes that somehow great work is being accomplished. The silent hand of God moves on, purifying the faculties of our soul, detaching us from possessions, people, and ourselves, raising us to various heights of prayer and increasing our capacity for love.

This dryness is like a spiritual anesthetic. It numbs our soul while the master sculptor shapes it into his image. We have no feeling of anything being accomplished. It is as if we were suspended between heaven and earth. We desire nothing of this world but we are still not ready for the pure air on the mountain of God. We wait, not always patiently, while we roam along unknown paths, thinking at times we are lost, but always finding a new path to take, a new cave to hide in, a dim light to follow.

God speaks to our souls, but we are so busy looking for him we do not hear his voice. We are desolate and become annoyed with ourselves and others. Not possessing the humility to realize we can do nothing of ourselves, we become feverishly active, perform more good works, read books, and distract ourselves from the emptiness that fills our souls.

Without realizing it, we are actually running away from the fire and into the cold, dark night. Our souls are restless for the warmth of his love and we do all we can to bring back past consolations. Our memory serves us well by recalling what used to be and we look back with great longing, convinced that somehow we are being chastised for some weakness or frailty.

This is not to say that dryness is not caused by lukewarmness, because it often is, but we must examine ourselves to judge the cause. We cannot torment our souls with scruples and doubts.

If our dry spell causes us pain, increases our thirst for God, makes us strive for virtue, and during prayer makes every other thought outside of God distasteful to us, then we can assume that the dryness we experience is of God. God is calling us to a higher form of prayer and a deeper union with himself.

Those who are lukewarm do not miss his presence; they do not imitate his virtues, and their prayer time, if any, is spent in willful distractions geared towards their own pleasure and convenience. For these souls we pray. We ask God for the grace of perseverance for ourselves so we do not fall away from his love and mercy. In order to better understand the power and beauty of spiritual dryness, we will look at its various aspects and try to reap the fruit of this call to greater things.

TEN

What Dryness Is

"SEE WHERE HE STANDS behind our wall. He looks in at the window, He peers through the lattice" (Sg 2:9).

In the beginning of our spiritual life God floods our souls with consolations, but before long his love demands that we rise above the feeling level and adore him "in spirit and truth."

So begins a kind of hide-and-seek. As the sacred writer records, God stands "behind a wall" blocked from our view, but he often "peers through the window" to give us a glimpse of his beautiful face. At other times it is as if a "lattice" were between the soul and God; we see him and yet we do not.

In this state of finding yet not finding, the soul is content with at least a little consolation. It becomes aware of his presence even though that presence is obscured by the things of this world and the frailties of human nature. In the past, meditations were a sheer joy and the soul believed that it had arrived at perfect peace. Its passions were in control and prayer was a glorious experience.

It is easy to be virtuous under these conditions. God lifts us out of ourselves and carries us along with ease. Our inner selves, enjoying the consolations of God, are so rapt in the sweetness of his presence that there is little chance of a permanent change. The presence of all goodness is like a magnet drawing us to himself; our weaknesses and passions are not gone, only dormant. They sleep while we are free to roam the realms of love in peace.

This state of soul cannot last for long. We have been given the grace to participate in the very nature of God. To fulfill this God-given role we must become more and more like him. We cannot do this if we inordinately cling to the emotions of our human nature.

Dryness of the Mind

In our daily life human love rests for the most part on a sense level, but since God is spirit we must communicate with him on a spirit-to-spirit level. We must be detached from the world and ourselves and seek him for himself alone. It is for this purpose that Jesus tells us "every branch that does bear fruit the Father prunes to make it bear even more" (Jn 15:2). It is those who are putting forth great effort to become like Jesus that God plunges into the darkness of dryness and into an awareness of their imperfections. So begins the purification of our faculties—memory, understanding, and will—and the beginning of our ascent to the mountain of holiness.

The faculty that is of great help in our meditations is our memory. It can recall incidents in the life of Jesus and picture them to our minds and make meditation a sheer delight. It is easy to recall Jesus in the agony in the garden and imagine ourselves kneeling beside him and consoling him in his hour of need. We may be content to lovingly look at him in his fear and feel his pain.

Our memory can serve us in a beautiful way during a meditation by bringing back the words of Jesus, his gestures, and his beautiful face. This use of memory and imagination can be of tremendous help by giving us a strong motive for following Jesus. It can fire us with zeal for his glory and inspire us to work for the salvation of souls.

The memory excites our emotions and our senses. Both virtue and sin can find a home in our memory and drive us to sanctity or damnation. Our five senses, prodded on by our reason, can lead us to heroic deeds of valor or black despair. Our wills, strong and powerful, can become so weak that we are "reeds shaken by the wind."

In a state of dryness, however, God purifies all three of these faculties in order to raise them up to the level of Jesus. When Paul asked us to "put on the mind of Christ," he was speaking of a purification initiated by God that raises our faculties to a spiritual plane. This purification is one we must accept, endure, and courageously persevere in as long as God wills it.

The first faculty to feel the pruning of the Father is our memory. It is as if all things good and holy were blanked out of our minds. We find meditation not only impossible but even distasteful. We endure this state for a few days thinking it will pass as all other trials do, but when the days pass on to weeks and months, sometimes into years, our intellect tells us we are wasting our time.

It is at this state of soul that the evil spirits, who realize the importance of dryness, tempt us to give up prayer, or torture us with the thought that some past sin has incurred God's anger upon us and he has left us to our miserable selves. Only the grace of God keeps us from despairing, for he gives us enough light and courage to continue praying despite the dryness inside and the assaults of the evil one outside.

Another phenomenon occurs in this state of soul: an exaggerated view of our weaknesses, faults, and imperfections that we have long accepted and fought against. They become so big that they engulf our souls like a huge monster. Those with whom we live or work become annoying and unbearable. It is as if the whole world were determined to destroy us. Sometimes sickness besets us and this, too, is borne with impatience and fear.

We are so engulfed in the pain of dryness and the avalanche of trials that we are under the impression we fight alone, unloved by God and distressed by our neighbors.

It is at this point that we don't do the things we want to do and do the things we don't want to do (Rom 7:19). What we fail to see is God's loving hand guiding us and leading us gently up the mountain of holiness. We *feel* so unholy, wicked, and lonely that God and his kingdom are far removed from our hearts. There is such a difference between his infinite holiness and our poor distressed souls that all we feel is unclean.

Our intellect, reasoning on a human level, keeps telling us that sanctity is not for us. It is obviously for those who have fortitude to accomplish great deeds and possess great talents and gifts.

As if to add fuel to the fire, our wills begin to vacillate and are confused as to the course to take. Our ability to accomplish anything on a spiritual level is difficult. A "do-nothing" attitude grips our souls and lukewarmness tries to wrap its arms around us.

It is nearly impossible for the soul to see how any good could come from this state of mind. But if the soul perseveres in its prayers and acts of virtue in spite of how it feels, it will soon begin to realize that its purification is good and freedom of spirit will be its reward.

Even though distractions plague its prayer time, the soul calmly returns to its seeking of the Lord as soon as it notices those distractions. The danger here is that the soul may seek consolations by deliberate distractions. Meditative reading is put aside and the soul spends the whole time of prayer reading a book that gives it consolation but little fervor. The shortening of prayer time is a real danger, for the fear of "wasting time" takes hold of the soul. As it seeks more action, the good works that bring consolation replace prayer time and the soul falls prey to great danger.

It is important to persevere in praying, even in lengthening the time of prayer, for the purification of dryness far outweighs the few consolations the soul derives from active works that distract it. To refuse to accept dryness is to refuse growth in the spiritual life. It is the vertical beam of our daily cross.

This is not to say that everyone suffers from dryness in the same way or length of time. Some souls suffer little from this type of purification and God can and often does lead them to great sanctity.

Jesus compared the Spirit to a wind when he spoke to Nicodemus, "Do not be surprised when I say: You must be born from above. The wind blows wherever it pleases; you hear its sound, but you cannot tell where it comes from or where it is going. That is how it is with all who are born of the Spirit" (Jn 3:7-8). The Sanctifier of our souls leads each one in a different way. It is not our duty to question how or why. We need only to trust his guidance of our souls, and if "dryness" is our constant companion, it is *our way*—the way of faith, of trust, of love.

Dryness sharpens every faculty. It forces us to great degrees of hope when our memory and imagination are dulled. It increases our faith for we must see him as he is and believe his Word. It strengthens our will by making it follow his commandments and imitate his virtues.

Our faculties seek this Lord as a deer seeks running water, and they constantly look out for him in an effort to find him. "Have you seen him whom my heart loves?" (Sg 3:3), the soul repeats over and over as it does all in its power to find what it feels it has lost.

As the soul is not aware of the life-giving blood flowing through its body, neither is it aware of the life-giving grace increasing in itself through the quiet flow of dryness.

Detachment is one of the greatest works of dryness. It is great because it is detaching us from ourselves and not from things. Things are comparatively easy to give up when we feel the loving arms of God around us. We are strangely very much aware of ourselves at this time. Although we enjoy the presence of God, it is the joy *we* are experiencing that occupies our mind and heart. So conscious are we of our sweet feelings that the loss of consolation causes us great pain. A void is created, but how often that void is more an absence of ourselves from feelings rather than an absence from his presence.

Our faith tells us that God is always present to us and by grace he is in our souls. Dryness then forces us to live by what faith teaches rather than what our feelings make us desire. Unless God bestows upon us the searing power of dryness we shall forever be swayed by emotional feelings designed to prod us on but never capable of changing us.

How true is the passage from the Song of Songs, "Catch the foxes for us, the little foxes that make havoc of the vineyards, for our vineyards are in flower" (2:15). Truly the soul is ready to bloom in the presence of its Creator but first those attachments, imperfections, and weaknesses must be overcome. The soul must be free to live in the presence of its Lord at all times. Its memory must be calmed and controlled, its intellect raised above itself in pure faith, and its will strong enough to follow in the footsteps of the Master.

How beautiful is the cross that brings about such marvelous changes in the soul. How grateful should we be to God for his patience with us even though we struggle against his providence and guidance. Let us not become giddy as we climb the mountain of holiness and forget our goals, our desires, and our way. If we ask God for sanctity we must believe that he has heard our prayer, and everything in our moment-to-moment existence is designed by him for that end.

Jesus has promised that when the Father sees us bearing fruit he will prune us so we may bear more fruit. It is by dryness again that God purifies our hearts. Our love, like his, must be pure and unselfish. It is in this area that dryness does its most glorious work.

Dryness of the Heart

Although our minds find it difficult to pray or concentrate on spiritual things during aridity, it is bearable when we have at least some knowledge of the love God has for us. Our striving to pray and practice virtue in the midst of dryness gives us some assurance that we do love God or we would not endure this trial. And so it is that a knowledge of God's love for us and of our love for him becomes the strong rope that we cling to as we climb the mountain of holiness.

But one day this prop is also taken away and our hearts are left without the last sign of love. The special assurance is gone and we feel the cold wind of the heights. Only the elements remain to strengthen and purify our hearts of all self-indulgence and selfish love.

We are offered the opportunity to love God for himself without expecting anything in return. We are given the chance of loving him when there are no manifest gifts and no consolations to encourage us. We are bereft of any feeling of love, and the desire for this sweet gift wells up in our hearts only to be disappointed by no response.

Now we stand alone before the majesty of God, and the brightness of that light makes us recoil at the difference between us. We feel unloved and unloving. When dryness attacked our minds there was at least a shred of love residing in our hearts, but now that is gone and we are forced to love only because we want to.

We are so accustomed to love on a human level that we find loving God for himself either impossible or beyond our capabilities. We tend to love those who appeal to us, render us a service, or are good to us. To the degree they perform these various services, we love them.

We often say that this particular person is our best friend. Usually this means that that person has the same goals, ambitions, likes, and dislikes as we. This friend makes us feel at ease in his presence and so we are fond of his company. What we most often like is the consolation afforded us. This is why in times of trial, sickness, or hardship, some friends drift apart and find each other boring.

However, a true friend loves us in every possible circumstance or trial. In fact, differences deepen our friendship because true love is fed by sacrifice.

Because God is spirit, invisible and all-perfect, our relationship with him is often built on the "rich uncle" concept that he has everything to give and we have only to receive. That we have anything to give upsets our theology and increases our responsibility. Any friendship not based on a mutual giving will not last. Selfish love cannot exist between friends for very long, and if that love is the basis of our relationship to God, it is a disaster. Yet to love on a selfish level is so basic to our nature. We tend to love him on the same level as we love our neighbor—for what he does or can give us.

Dryness of heart—that purifying cross—cleanses our love of all selfishness and raises it to a level of unselfish love. We begin to love freely, because we want to, because God is all-lovable. The wrenching of self from our prayer time with God, by this inability to feel any love in our hearts, raises us to the level of the new commandment. On this level of prayer, we pray and love God for himself alone, not for the gifts or consolations he gives us. This new attitude and degree of love extends itself to our neighbor and we begin to love him in the same way God loves us—unselfishly.

Only through the pain of dryness—where we decrease and he increases—can we begin to love God in the way he wishes us to love. When we pray we are doing so on our will power, for our poor human nature receives no compensation for its efforts.

Faith tells us that God is present when we pray and hope tells us he listens, but only love makes us continue to pray when darkness, boredom, and even disgust fill our souls to overflowing. Only a *true* love will persevere in praying despite darkness and confusion.

Must God try us so? Yes, because he wants us to love as he loves and be holy as he is holy. Through his grace, his presence, and his love in our souls, he cries out for us to love him as he is and to be so attuned to his Spirit that the mere whisper of his voice enkindles our hearts with love.

This is difficult for our human nature to understand. Human love is associated with feelings, such as the feeling of benevolence, the feeling of confidence, the feeling of filial or paternal love, the love born of friendship, and the love that makes a man and woman desire to live together in a state of marriage. All these kinds of love are connected in various ways to feelings and so it is natural for us to think that our love for God should be on the same level.

This conviction is strengthened by the fact that when we first found the Lord we experienced a tremendous emotional uplift. Our hearts sang the praises of God with great enthusiasm. We bore pain with joy, and if misfortune overtook us we accepted it with a flare of detachment we never experienced before.

When God began to prune that which was so good in the beginning, it was natural to think that consolations would continue. We expected to work hard and give up much—but the fires of his love, so sweet to our taste, would never leave us.

The knowledge that his presence never leaves us adds to the cross of dryness because we think that presence must be felt. We are slow to understand that God wants us to have both a yearning and an assurance of his presence—but in faith. His presence dwelling in our hearts increases our capacity for love. His grace, ever gratuitous and independent of our good actions, increases our degree of love and permits us to return love for love. His love in us, as we are emptied of self, becomes our love for him. We begin to love him with the love of the Spirit ever dwelling in our hearts.

Through the purification of dryness of heart, the Holy Spirit becomes the greatest love in our souls. We begin to love God with our will. We choose to love him, to spend some time with him, to prefer him to ourselves. It is a hard lesson to learn, but God slowly guides our poor hearts towards himself and frees us of all the attachments that keep us from giving ourselves to him totally.

Dryness takes away the wrong kind of love in our hearts and leaves the heart empty and ready for a divine influx of grace, a greater participation in the divine nature, a purer, unadulterated love, a love that is God himself.

Like all operations, this is extremely painful because it strikes at the very source of feelings, consolations, and the sense of well-being that we call happiness. It cuts deep into our selfish love and ruthlessly carves it out. It is when we gaze up to the Father in anguish of heart, lonely and empty, that the Spirit of love accepts the ashes of our human love and begins his work of transformation. It is time for Jesus to bear fruit in our souls.

ELEVEN

The Fruits of Dryness

Detachment

Perhaps one of the first fruits the Spirit bears in our souls through the purification of dryness is detachment.

The people and things we are attached to are the things we love selfishly. We find comfort and consolation in them, and in proportion as our souls cling to these feelings, in that proportion we are attached.

Attachments to spiritual experiences lead to spiritual gluttony. We seek consolations, become disconsolate without them, jealous of those who possess them, and are never satisfied with God's plan in our lives. We demand from God or bring upon ourselves consolations, the fruit of which is a repugnance for suffering in any form. We run from the pruning hand of the Father, and in so doing deprive our souls of the consolations at the heights of prayer. We are not willing to give up the sweetness of being aware of the presence of God for the growth of faith in our lives.

This unwanted and unappreciated dryness of soul brings about the virtue we do not have the courage to exercise—detachment. It has the power to strip us of the things we desire and covet most of all—feelings. By the stripping down of feelings, dryness leaves our souls open to objective thinking, clear thinking, and an unselfish concern for others.

If we are patient with our dryness, we will see clearly how it separates our personal feelings from prayer and various incidents of daily life. The constant demand made upon us during prayer habituates us to unselfish living. If we are strong enough to love and commune with God without feelings, we shall do the same with our neighbor. We shall love that neighbor with a detached love. This means we make *loving* more important than *being loved* in return.

The soul realizes that in this short journey of life, it has the opportunity to manifest its love for Jesus by comforting him, being zealous for his glory rather than its own, and growing in that Godlike love whose seed was planted in the soul at baptism.

This is the time to console Jesus by a perfect union of our will with his—a loving acceptance of the work of his Spirit in our souls.

There are so many things in life to which we become attached. We are encouraged by the world to possess as many things as possible. The concept of poverty of spirit is foreign and unacceptable to the world and it is abhorrent to the demons.

It is necessary then for God to place us in a position of detachment—a kind of involuntary renunciation—that will prune our souls and lead them to freedom. We are slow to detach ourselves and when we manage some kind of voluntary detachment, we begin by doing without the things we care for the least. Those things dear to our hearts we rationalize into keeping or we leave them till last.

The Spirit of God assists us in this painful mortification by giving us a dryness of soul that does not find pleasure or comfort in anything. Even nature, beautiful and majestic as it comes from the power of God, leaves us cold and unimpressed.

The love of friends only makes us realize how much we miss his presence. The thought of past spiritual experiences, when we were aware of his love and goodness, only creates a greater void that nothing can fill.

The more we reach out to creatures to fill the void in our hearts, the deeper that void becomes. Like the bride in the Song of Songs, we cry out to everyone, "Have you seen him whom my heart loves?" (Sg 3:3). What a blessing that God's pruning does not permit us to find comfort in anyone or anything! Surely, we would cling to the least comfort and be willing to forego our climb up the mountain of holiness if we could find solace in creation.

We are so caught up in our own miseries that our soul becomes very much aware of itself. As in bodily pain, when the mind focuses itself almost entirely on one small part of the body, the soul becomes painfully aware of its finiteness and its total inability to accomplish any good work on its own. Now it is that it becomes detached from the *desire* for consolation. The sight of its limitations forces the soul to depend entirely upon God and his grace to bear fruit. It has begun to realize that without him it can do nothing (Jn 15:5).

It is important at this stage for the soul to possess a healthy self-love. If it does not, the consciousness of its imperfections, weaknesses, and frailties, plus the dryness, will bring the soul to near despair. By healthy self-love is meant a realization of the soul's value and uniqueness before God. So much is the individual soul loved by the Father, that he gave his only Son for its salvation and eternal happiness. It must understand and make a distinction then between *who* it is and what it does.

The weakness of which it is guilty can be changed and transformed by the love of Jesus and the grace of his Spirit. The realization of the dignity of the soul after baptism must never be smothered under the frailties of its nature. The individual is a child of God, an heir to the kingdom, and the thought of God's infinite mercy in its regard must ever keep the soul elevated above itself.

If we cannot love ourselves as masterpiece of God's power and at the same time hate the sins we commit, we shall be unable to relate to our neighbor in love. When we find sin we shall hate the sinner and fail to make the distinction between our neighbor and his weaknesses. It will be difficult to love that neighbor in the way God loves him because that neighbor must be near-perfect before he can receive our love. The commandment will be merely a distant ideal.

When we are detached from ourselves we suddenly find that loving our neighbor is easy. We no longer make distinctions between those we "like" and those we "love." The selfish motives that attracted us to some and repelled us from others have been swallowed up in the chasm of our own nothingness. Jesus has filled the void created and sustained by dryness. His love in our hearts reaches out to love everyone.

Humility

One of the most painful lessons that dryness teaches us is the spirit of humility. Our total helplessness in the face of our inability to pray can almost annihilate our pride. We may rebel against this feeling of inadequacy, but if we accept it we can make a giant stride towards a spirit of humility.

Because the humility that is the fruit of dryness is not self-imposed, the soul is guarded against a false humility which says it can do nothing of itself but does not really believe it. Neither is this humility the fruit of persecution or misunderstanding. It is, therefore, a safeguard against the resentment that often accompanies the clashes of personality traits in our relationships with others.

It is a crushing blow to our pride to realize we must wait upon the Lord to pray well or to pray at all. As often as we read Jesus' statement that without him we can do nothing, this hardly reaches an experiential stage in our lives. When we kneel before him, helpless, dry, and in a state of confusion, we begin to feel our finite condition. A reality of life becomes an experience for us: without him we can do nothing, not even pray.

It is good to have an intellectual awareness of our dependence upon God, to understand how great he is and how very small we are in his sight. But when our very bones feel the weight of his holiness upon us and we are conscious of our sinful condition, then we pass from knowing *about* God to knowing God. The former is knowledge, the latter experience.

While the essence of dryness is a lack of feeling, the consciousness of one's unworthiness, with all the weaknesses of human nature strong and operative, is very much a feeling but one not to our liking. We try to run away from the feeling of our nothingness that overwhelms us, but we cannot. The soul's awareness of its wretched condition can do more to its pride in five minutes than a thousand humiliations in a lifetime.

Not only does the soul possess a new sense of its dependence upon God but its self-knowledge is increased to an alarming degree. Every fault is magnified and the soul sees weaknesses within it that never before came to the surface. This self-knowledge is the very root of humility; when the soul sees itself as it really is and then gazes at the infinite God who loves it, the reality of the vast difference between them engenders humility, provided that this knowledge is accepted with a deep sense of gratitude.

This gratitude is not only for the light given but for the gratuitous love bestowed upon the lowly soul by the infinite God. The reality of God's personal love for a poor weak human being sends the soul into transports of joy, even though the feeling of dryness fills the soul with consternation and its weaknesses overwhelm it. In its very depths, there begins a quiet acceptance of itself and of God, and a determined effort evolves that drives the soul on to a deeper love in a spirit of sacrifice.

The soul slowly understands what humility of heart means. It does not feel crushed or broken but it is overwhelmed by a sense of its sinful condition, of its capacity for evil, and the thin thread that separates it from God whose "power is at its best in weakness" (2 Cor 12:9).

It is no longer discouraged by its tendencies towards sin; it is more surprised at what it does not do, and implores the grace of God ever to stay in his favor. Its striving for perfection becomes more interior, and with the effort to overcome exterior faults it tries to improve its motives. It strives to be gentle not only in action but in *heart*. There comes to the soul a realization that but for the grace of God it is capable of any sin. It therefore is more humble in its attitude towards the weak and more gentle when correction is necessary.

The inner conviction of the soul's capacity for evil, though it ever strives for holiness, prevents that arrogance that finds fault with others. Only the soul that "feels" it is nothing but keeps its eyes on Jesus can begin the climb up the mountain of perfection. The soul at this stage does not expect much of itself since its self-knowledge has been increased. It does expect much from God, however, because it realizes the real source of its power. Thus the soul learns to harmonize self-knowledge that expects little good from itself, and hope in God from whom it expects everything.

Dryness again becomes the pivot point for a balance of opposite emotions—deep repentance and great love, fear of the Lord and confidence, distrust of one's own strength and hope in his power, fear of one's own weaknesses and trust in his grace.

Though failure, pain, and suffering humble our minds, it is the power of dryness that God uses to humble our hearts. Jesus warned us that it was from men's hearts that evil arose, and so it is our hearts that God purifies and humbles so that the seed of evil, sown by the enemy, may not take root.

Patience

One of the most difficult virtues for our human nature to acquire is patience: that ability to wait in peace.

There are few of us who possess patience on a natural level, for our modern world has conditioned us to perform every duty in record time. We purchase whatever food is instant, and whatever mode of travel is the faster. Though we complain of boredom we are in a hurry to get anywhere we are going, and then we rush when we arrive so that we can return in the shortest possible time.

We are victims of a hurried society—part of a perpetual merry-go-round that is constantly in motion but never leaves its place. Our feet run on an invisible treadmill that keeps us out of breath while we rush from one activity to another. Loud music and clashing sounds keep our nerves frayed and our emotions at a high pitch. Like the voice of a circus barker crying, "Hurry, Hurry, Hurry," the world keeps us all in some kind of motion so we do not have time to think, pray, or otherwise get our wits together.

The Holy Spirit cannot work in this din and clamor. As Elijah realized, the Spirit is like a gentle breeze, quietly inspiring, and speaking softly in the silence of our hearts. Rushing, noise, uneasiness, lack of self-control, and the constant move towards more and more action, drowns his voice and nullifies his inspirations.

While we feel impelled to run, run, run, the Spirit moves slowly and quietly, and we end up further and further away from our only source of peace and contentment. As we insist on moving faster and faster, his pace seems slower and slower to our whirling minds.

We have not lost God or religion—we only possess such a small amount of both that in a hurried society we cannot stop long enough to see what we possess. Perhaps we are afraid that if we stop we will be forced to take inventory and face the truth: we possess very little living water.

When we begin to realize there is a vacuum in our lives—a vacuum only God can fill—we find Jesus in a new way. We are aware of our tremendous need of him in our daily lives. The joy of finding him is accompanied by a desire for holiness. It is in this desire for holiness that we carry some of our worldly concepts and demands for "instant" results.

We are so accustomed to the rush of modern-day living and

so inebriated with the desire for holiness that there seems to be some reason for our becoming holy instantly. Because the world is in great need and much of our lives have been wasted in dissipation, the logical conclusion is that our holiness must be not only different from the past but also be accomplished in the fastest possible way.

We can repent in a split second but the changing of our lives and the conquering of human frailties is the job of a lifetime. This is where patience matures into peaceful serenity.

It is the work of dryness to bring about these spiritual wonders. Dryness teaches the soul to wait on the Lord and to learn that if it waits with impatience, the dryness becomes unbearable.

Inner patience is necessary to persevere in our quest for humility of heart. If we cannot possess our soul in patience we shall find it difficult to endure the time it takes to change, to empty ourselves, and to become generous and detached.

Without patience, holiness will take on impossible dimensions and, like the seed sown on a layer of thin soil, our desires will sprout but never grow and take root. It is necessary, then, that we appreciate the beauty of God's pruning in our spiritual lives. We must wait and grow during our time of dryness, grow in patience so we may bear another necessary fruit—perseverance.

Perseverance

In the Gospels of Matthew and Mark, Jesus tells us, "you will be hated by all men on account of my name." He then adds a statement that makes it clear we must persevere in our seeking of God. Isolated acts of goodness are not enough to become holy. He said, "The man who stands firm to the end will be saved" (Mt 10:22; Mk 13:13).

The words "to the end" and "will be" indicate a future event. Now all men are saved by the precious blood of Jesus but not all men accept the call to be a son of God. There are those who reject God totally at the hour of death and refuse God's forgiveness. Jesus said that this sin would not be forgiven.

No sin is greater than God's mercy, and God extends that mercy to everyone up to his last breath. It is the soul who then rejects God: God never rejects the soul.

Man does not reach that state of total rejection overnight or by one act of sin. Rejection of God is something gradual and is made up of little acts of lukewarmness, selfishness, nurtured resentments, cherished hatreds, and egotistical pride—the kind of pride that never admits a weakness, never acknowledges a fault, and is never sorry for past sins. A constant diet of these little and big faults leads the soul further and further from a dependence upon God as the giver of all good things.

To continue rejecting these tendencies we need the virtue of perseverance. We need that strong determination that makes us forge ahead no matter what obstacles and failures we face.

Dryness of soul makes us strong in perseverance because we must exercise this virtue if we are to continue in our prayer life. Perseverance places our love, virtues, and good deeds on a will level as opposed to the emotional level on which we usually live.

Most of us become lax in our resolutions because we do not *feel* the enthusiasm of a newborn Christian—one who has just received the good news. But unless the gospel message always remains fresh, good and new to our souls, our perseverance will be short-lived, our conversion insincere, and our resolutions weak.

We know that it is difficult to continue on a course of action that is not approved of by the world, or to live by an invisible reality that is opposed to the greed and permissiveness of the world. St. Paul realized how important it was to stand and persevere in our good resolutions. Repeatedly he encourages the Christians to keep doing good and praying much in spite of persecutions. They could not rest on the fact that they had heard the good news and accepted it.

He tried to give the Hebrews motives for persevering and said, "You and I are not the sort of people who draw back and are lost by it [suffering]; we are the sort who keep faithful until our souls are saved" (Heb 10:39).

When Paul told the Romans to be careful and to remember their glorious destiny, he reminded them that, "We must hope to be saved since we are not saved yet—it is something we must wait for with patience" (Rom 8:25).

But lest they become discouraged, he told them that the Spirit would help them in their weakness. It was then that Paul gave a most beautiful description of the value of dryness in prayer: "When we cannot choose words in order to pray properly, the Spirit himself expresses our plea in a way that could never be put into words" (Rom 8:26). Paul realized by the past experience with men and the world and a deep realization of his own weaknesses that man had to persevere in praying and in doing good and had to do this to the very end of his life.

Paul assured us that if we keep praying no matter how difficult it is or how dry we feel, "God who knows everything in our hearts knows perfectly well what the Spirit means, and that the pleas of the saints expressed by the Spirit are according to the mind of God" (Rom 8:27).

Yes, if we persevere and remember with St. Peter that we must be "calm but vigilant, because your enemy, the devil, is prowling round like a roaring lion looking for someone to eat" (1 Pt 5:8), and if we recall with Paul that God turns everything to good for those who love him (Rom 8:28), then we shall stand firm to the end (Rom 8:28).

Dryness is a great aid towards the strengthening of our will, determination, and effort towards holiness of life. It is that purifying instrument in the hand of God that appears cold, dark, and painful but in reality is warm, bright, and healing to our imperfect spirits.

TWELVE

Prayer without Ceasing

I N THE DEPTHS of the human soul is a yearning for God that
will never be satisfied in this life. Because of this yearning,
Jesus has given us the command to "pray without ceasing"
(Lk 18:1).

We yearn to be united to God, to live in his company, to
speak to him as a friend speaks to a friend. We desire to think as
he thinks and to love as he loves. These desires and yearnings,
constantly living side by side with our weak sinful nature,
create contradictions, dilemmas, and anxieties too complex
for us to solve. Holiness and corruption live together as an
uneven team, each pulling and tugging at our soul in order to
sway it to their respective paths.

We spend much time planning a course of action, not unlike
those in worldly pursuits. We sit down and devise various
means to overcome ourselves, categorize our virtues and
faults, read the lives of the saints, and then determine upon a
course of action and a way of life that will transform us into
images of Jesus. All this is good and admirable, but soon a
period of dryness shatters our plans and guides us on a course
we would not choose for ourselves.

Looking at our virtues suddenly seems futile, for dryness
has taught us that we can do nothing by ourselves. Our
weaknesses seem multiplied, and the lives of the saints, so
edifying in the past, make us realize that by comparison, we are

like ants looking at giants. Our best-laid plans have come to naught and we gaze at God with a clogged mind and an empty heart.

At this time, only one thing rises above everything else in our lives, and that is a burning thirst for God. It is both sweet and bitter—sweet because the very thought of God fills us with love, and bitter because the more we love, the more we thirst, and the more we thirst the more empty we feel. It is a sweet contradiction and a happy dilemma.

This state is sweet yet bitter, peaceful yet confused, happy yet sad, restful yet yearning, tranquil yet painful. It is the state of a pilgrim content with the difficult journey because he anticipates the end in view.

Without realizing it, we begin to pray without ceasing. Thirst for God and emptiness of heart slowly condition the soul to seek God every moment. This seeking puts the soul in a state of prayer that sets no time limits. Because the dryness within is constant, the effort to alleviate it must be continuous, and it is this persevering effort that prepares the soul for unceasing prayer. Detachment, humility, a thirst for God, and great determination give the soul that necessary thrust forward to arrive at a state of prayer that is constant rather than intermittent.

Only one thing is necessary: a companionship with God that is reverent, filled, deep, and burning with love, a love that is enhanced every moment by the nearness of his presence, his action in our lives, his mercy in our souls, his tenderness in our sorrows, his strength in our pain. Dryness dispels the cobwebs covering our minds and the superfluities that keep us entangled in a maze of nothingness. We are free to roam the limitless realms of his love, which are ever there to be grasped in a new way.

This seeking, grasping, possessing, and then seemingly losing, his presence keeps us striving towards him in a peaceful attitude of prayer. It is here that we realize the necessity and the possibility of continuous prayer.

In all the other stages that dryness thrusts us into, we learned forms of prayer. We called out to God for mercy, meditated on his life, gazed at him in an act of silent love, and said many short prayers that were darts of love to remind him of our desire to be all his.

These many kinds of prayer become a habit and, coupled with the freedom that dryness brings to our souls, we find ourselves able to use one and then another with great freedom. We are suddenly detached from forms of prayer—free in his Spirit—free to use wordy or wordless prayers, ready to silently gaze or joyously proclaim our love for him, ready for consolation or desolation, ready for sickness or health, ready to see Jesus in our neighbor unhampered by his faults, ready to do his will and prefer him to all things.

We finally realize that saying prayers is only a means—a necessary means—to continuous prayer. Prayer in itself is a constant companionship with God as Father, Savior, and Lord, an uninterrupted awareness of his presence—consciously when we think or speak of him, and unconsciously when we do everything for love of him.

Unceasing prayer is to love God so much that when we are not speaking to him we speak *of* him, and when we can do neither, our heart rests in an awareness of his presence, doing whatever we do *for* him.

Jesus told us that not all those who say "Lord, Lord" will enter the Kingdom. We begin to understand what this means for we realize now that we are praying when we love him, but we do not necessarily love him when we are *saying* prayers. The intensity of our life of continuous prayer will vary as our love is deep, our hope is sure, and our faith is living. It takes faith to see Jesus in order to speak to him; it takes hope to speak to others of him; and it takes great love to desire nothing but him.

The one thing necessary has become the prayer without ceasing. The soul has shed its complexities and wrapped itself in the simple cloak of unity with the Trinity in love and peace. It is truly free.

Purified of some of the imperfections in our souls, we can better see Jesus in our neighbor. We can see the suffering Redeemer in the needs of the world, and because we possess him, we can reach out in an unselfish gesture of love and concern.

We can think of others rather than ourselves. We can give, though nothing is given in return. We can love, though we experience coldness. We can rejoice in the midst of pain. We can see the Father, as Jesus did, in every circumstance, because we are more aware of Jesus in people—Jesus in suffering, Jesus in want, Jesus in desolation, Jesus in joy, Jesus in distress, and Jesus in pain.

When we begin to empty ourselves and to listen to the silent presence of the Father in creation, then we slowly see Jesus, the Father's perfect image, in the souls of human beings. Realizing our own misery, through the searing light of aridity, we no longer look for perfection in others, but only the suffering Redeemer in need—a need that only we can alleviate.

At the last day, he will ask us if we saw him—hungry, thirsty, sick, and in prison, and, having seen him, did we reach out to lift his burden? Were we loving to the unloved, generous to the selfish, humble to the proud, compassionate towards the hard of heart, and merciful toward sinners?

It will come as a complete surprise to many that what we "rendered to the least, we rendered to him." In the same way, we will be surprised to find that all creation was a mere shadow of his presence—a constant reminder, so often forgotten, of the Father's love, providence, and power. We shall wonder at how close God was to us during our lifetime, and we shall be stunned into awesome silence when we see how much we have done, or neglected to do, to Jesus in our neighbor. We will understand what marvels of grace were wrought by his purifying silence.

THIRTEEN

Our Loving Guest

BECAUSE THE GOD OF LOVE breathed a soul into our body, love is an integral part of our nature. We seek love even in our mother's womb. A baby reaches up for the warm embrace of its mother, and the reassuring hand of its father. Somehow, it knows the difference between them, for love discerns the various kinds of love and seeks to increase itself from moment to moment.

Our life would be colorless and lifeless without the love of family and friends—the love that makes us stand tall and unafraid, because it gives us assurance, acceptance, courage, strength, and confidence.

All of this is natural because it is inborn and inherited. Though we cannot describe it, we do *feel* it. We express love by touch and emotions, a light in our eyes, and sweet words on our tongue. It is a spark that we feel and cling to, a light that burns, and an emotion to rest in.

The God of love created us to be like himself—love. Man, however, turned that love towards himself through pride, and then he ceased to love. He began to hate, to be selfish, deceitful, and arrogant.

It became increasingly difficult to love as his Creator loved, with a compassionate and universal love. He began to love only those who loved him or rendered him a service. He could not persevere in loving when that love demanded sacrifice, and so he found excuses not to love. It was then that human life was of little value, for without Godlike love, life was merely survival of the fittest.

To redeem us from this state of rebellion, the Father, who is infinite love, sent the perfect image of that love, his Son, to show us how real love thinks and acts. He would manifest the fruit of love in words and deeds. He would give us detailed examples of how love reacts under every joyful or painful circumstance. He would light our path, direct our steps, and lead us to the well of living water.

Men who lived with him wrote down his words and deeds, but, knowing how difficult it would be for us to remember everything we read, much less live by it, he told us not to worry for he would send his Spirit, and the Spirit would bring to mind everything he taught us. Love sent love to earth, and the Spirit of that love lives in our hearts to teach, to guide, to correct, to console, to fill, and to transform.

The Holy Spirit, whose presence is silent because it is within, sees our thoughts, hears our sighs, and fulfills our desires. The very breath of God breathes within us, for we are his living temple. He moves our will, but never interferes with its freedom. He corrects our weaknesses with gentle persuasion, and inspires our thoughts with holy desires and zealous works. He issues forth from the Father and the Son, and touches our souls with a beam of light that enlightens our minds, increases our faith, enlivens our hope, and sets our weak love aflame.

The good thoughts we have are mere whisperings of his gentle voice; our conscience, the prodding of his guidance; our desires for holiness, the sparks of his love; and the strength of our souls, the power of his omnipotence. He fills our souls with goodness, peace, love, joy, kindness, and mercy. We cannot say "Jesus is Lord" without him, nor can we embrace the cross with joy unless his mighty hand lifts it for us.

He warns us of occasions of sin by a gentle thought of danger. He instills a desire to set goals and work for the kingdom. He whispers words of love to speak to the Father, and deeds of valor to be accomplished for the Son. He watches over us as we sleep, and sets our feet on level ground as we begin a new day. As long as we do not evict him by sin, he lives in our souls to instill a spirit of love we never dreamed possible. We were created *to* love, but he transforms us *into* love, for he makes us as he is, and we become more and more like Jesus in thought and deed.

When St. Paul told us there were many gifts but the same Spirit, he was telling us that all the good we do, all the talents that manifest the Father's attributes, all the virtues that imitate Jesus, and all the thoughts that express love and kindness, come from the Holy Spirit in us. These good things come from him, for, as St. Paul tells us in his Epistle to the Galatians, love, peace, and joy come from the Holy Spirit. They are his fruit in us.

Our problem rests in the fact that we attribute these things to ourselves. Our part of sanctification is to give him freedom to work in us, give him our will to accomplish in us, and give him our heart to love with. He, and he alone, can bear the fruit of Jesus in our souls. He, and he alone, can bestow grace, for only God can give God to men. His very Spirit thinks through our thoughts, and breathes with our breath, because he delights to be with the children of men.

Like any friend who is a guest in our home, he will not force himself upon us. He comes to us at baptism and will remain with his gifts as long as we desire him to stay. Only our own will can drive him away, when we choose ourselves and sin in preference to him. God and the enemy cannot dwell in the same house at the same time. The noise and confusion of sin and selfishness drowns out his voice and drives him away.

The Silence of the Holy Spirit

Of our three silent guests, the Holy Spirit is the most silent, because his work is to change us, sanctify us, and transform us.

It is, by its very nature, a hidden work, so as not to interfere with our will, our personality, our talents, and our desires. If we are not attuned to his silent presence, we will think we make ourselves holy—so hidden, quiet, and gentle is his work in our souls. But as we accustom ourselves to listen to his silent whisperings, we are soon aware of how powerful and loving he is in us.

He it is who tears away the veils of imperfection that hide the presence of Jesus in our neighbor. His love, operating in us, reaches out to the needs of our neighbor. His strength gives us courage to fight the enemy, the world, and ourselves, that we may "put on the mind of Christ." He it is who teaches us to love with an unselfish love, even unto death. He it is who breathes into our frail bodies a new spirit, a new heart, and a new mind.

When we read scripture, his presence puts light where there was once darkness. When we are in sin, his voice instills feelings of repentance. When we find it impossible to love, he sends a spark from his fire to warm our cold hearts. When we are not sure which way to turn, he gives us discernment to see the best way, and then gives us courage to follow through. When we feel tied down by ambition and possessions, he instills a deep realization of the one thing necessary, and the futility of all passing things. And then, when our souls are in a vacuum, he fills them to overflowing with the sweetness of his love. He is always active in our souls, but in such a quiet, gentle, and humble way that sometimes we hardly know he is there.

Throughout his epistles, in places too numerous to count, St. Paul tells us how it was the Holy Spirit who guided him, calmed him, encouraged him, prayed in him, corrected him, led him to suffering and glory, dwelt within him, and finally transformed him into Jesus.

The silent presence of God's love, manifested in the humanity of his Son and the indwelling of his Spirit, raises us up to divine adoption as sons of God. As he hovered over the waters and created something out of nothing, so he hovers over us and dwells within us, to exert his omnipotence once more, and transform souls of finite creatures into Jesus.

Lest we stray from truth, because we are often hard of heart and confused in soul, he forever dwells in the church, to guide us to truth free of error, enlighten our consciences, and instruct our minds to see his revelations and his will.

He is our friend in need, our consolation in suffering, our solace in affliction, our light in darkness, our director in the ways of holiness, and our source of grace. He hides himself that we may be perfectly free to choose—and then manifests himself that we may have courage to carry on.

The Father's humility astounds us, as we see how hidden and silent he is in all his creation. The Son's humility amazes us, as we observe his gentle meekness in dealing with his creatures. The Spirit's humility confounds us, as we see how unpretentious and hidden is his guidance of our souls. And then the pride of man embarrasses us as we see our God so humble, hidden, and silent.

Before redemption, mankind could only relate to God as Creator and Lord. How wonderful that Jesus revealed there are three persons in one God. Now we can relate to God as Father and Friend, to Jesus as Savior and Spouse, and to the Spirit as Lover and Sanctifier. Now we are the recipients of the Father's compassion, the Son's precious blood, and the Spirit's grace. Now we can glorify the Father above us by becoming like Jesus, through the power of the Spirit within us. Now we can listen to the silent presence of the Father around us, and see the silent presence of the Son in our neighbor—because we possess their enlightening Spirit of love within us.

Living in That Secret Place

The real Christian lives in an atmosphere of prayer. For him, prayer is not a spiritual exercise that he performs on occasion, it is a way of life. There are times he says prayers, but those are the times he asks for the things he needs. Most of his time is spent in preparing himself to live in God as God lives in him.

He uses every occasion to lift his mind and heart to God and creates for himself a secret place, a place where he and his God dwell alone. His spiritual faculties are ever seeking opportunities to listen to the silent presence, to see the silent presence, and to possess that silent presence. His soul raises itself up to God like incense, enveloping itself in the cloud of his surrounding presence.

A Christian does not strain after God as one seeks a lost object; he merely becomes more and more aware of what he already possesses—his loving presence.

A Christian is a realist who fears neither suffering, pain, nor persecution, for he endures nothing alone. He does not seek riches or poverty, for he knows that both come from God and both can be used for his glory and the good of the kingdom.

A Christian is a young child in the midst of an old world, to witness to the joys of heaven on earth.

He is free in heart, to love friends and enemies alike—for his only goal is to be like the Father. He is free in mind, for he believes with humble acceptance the mysteries of God and revels in their magnitude and variety. His will is free, for his only desire is to unite himself to God. His love demands a union that brings the infinite and the finite together in an embrace of love.

A Christian has a sense of his Lord's presence though he does not often feel it. Though his soul is often sunk in doubt, it is never clouded by those doubts, for he accepts his limitations with quiet humility.

He wonders, as other men wonder, but he has someone to go to, to solve his problems, quiet his anxieties, discern his way, lighten his burdens, and share his pain.

A Christian has a power because he has a presence who is always with him. He is happy because he possesses the only source of joy. He is serene because he lives in the changeless one. He is strong in his weaknesses because he gives room for infinite strength to work through him.

A Christian lives and breathes in the silent presence of his Lord. He is humble in the success of his work, in imitation of the Father. He is humble in regard to his neighbor, in imitation of Jesus. He is humble in his love, in imitation of the Spirit.

He listens to the silent majesty of his Father's creative power in the world. He sees the silent, suffering redeemer in the hearts of all men. He experiences the silent presence of the Holy Spirit in the depths of his own being.

Yes, a Christian is alert to the silent presence. It does not matter to him whether he listens, sees, or experiences that presence in faith or ecstatic love. He seeks one thing—the enveloping presence of his Lord. Once he has found that presence, his whole life is spent in listening, seeing, and being aware of his silent presence.